Living Life
For You

IN LETTING YOUR KIDS GO AND BE GROWN,
YOU CAN REDISCOVER YOU

Living Life For You

IN LETTING YOUR KIDS GO AND BE GROWN, YOU CAN REDISCOVER YOU

LILA REYNA

ISBN: 978-1-7337407-0-8

Printed in the United States of America

www.LilaReyna.com

Contents

"Holding on is believing there's a past.
Letting go is knowing there's a future."

— Daphne Rose Kingma

THE JOURNEY

I don't know about you, but when I cradled my newborn in my arms, I must have missed the "What to expect when they up and leave the nest" handout. There's no step-by-step guide to follow when your adult child moves out and stops talking to you. Or when they know more than you do and suddenly your opinion carries little or no weight. Or when you need to prepare them for a successful move-out. Or when the house is empty and you realize your entire reality, your entire life, has been rudely disrupted.

Much emphasis in our society is placed on raising the young child, and for good reason, too. But in reality, motherhood doesn't stop when the kids move out, it just changes. And sometimes it can be even more challenging, because it's about finding the crazy balance between loving, trusting, and letting go.

Living Life for You is about accepting change and being aware of and accountable for your own happiness, because ready or not, it will happen—your children will grow up and leave, and you will be left staring into a mirror. That's when the gentle calling of your soul may beg the question, *Who am I, now?* It's a natural time in your life to reflect on what was, what is, and what is to be.

This book doesn't come from lofty heights. This book comes from experiences; from the tears, the joy, the challenges, the laughing, the trying, the failures and the successes from my own life and from the moms I've interviewed. I am not a doctor. I am not a therapist. But I have handled pain and hardship and I survived; I work with women on a daily basis, teaching self-defense and awareness, and I had the honor of interviewing over fifty moms for this book. And my own three children—although there were definitely rocky times—have grown into well-adjusted, happy adults.

At times we all face different struggles, and I wrote this book to offer some ideas, thoughts, stories, and inspiration from one mom to another. May it help you, in whatever way you need most, to let go of the past, accept the future, and embrace this inevitable change with open arms.

So, let's raise a glass, together, to all moms—may we share our tears, laughter, trials, and tribulations with each other. May we share our own experiences, reach out to each other, communicate, and learn from each other. And may you create the customized manual you need in order to live your own life with purpose and with passion—to live life for you.

Introduction

READY OR NOT

Motherhood is a special role for which I've given thanks for approximately 8,283 days. Not all these days were spectacular, though most of them were. But just when I got comfortable, and feeling pretty good in terms of figuring out selfless parenting—surviving my adolescents' sullenness, making four million meals a day, avoiding the kids' shoes and backpacks in the middle of the living room floor, pointing out (for the thousandth time) that the lights had been left on, and discovering which new driver in the house had forgotten to put gas in the car after they had it out—my kids just up and left our household to go live on their own, either to attend college or enlist in the Air Force.

OMG!

It's true that a mother's job is to teach her children not to need her anymore, but no one mentioned the hardest part of that job would be accepting its actual success. Yes, *of course* I actively encouraged my children to become more independent so that one day they would be capable of managing the next chapter of their lives. Still, the loss of having them in the household on a daily basis was so overwhelming; the actual experience of letting go nothing short of painful. I went from wearing a "Wonder Mom" cape and fulfilling all my children's needs to suddenly having no children at home needing my constant care and attention. I felt naked without that cape, and daily life felt like . . . a void.

One day, my home was full of noise and steady commotion. Then, as abruptly as they had arrived way back when, the children were gone. Without the chaotic diversions of raising children, I suddenly found myself with time to reflect: *What did I do right? Where did I fail? And who will show up to help me out with the transition?*

Concerns popped up one by one—often in the middle of the night when I couldn't sleep. Would I be able to keep a healthy line of communication open with my adult children? And even more pressing, now that the house was silent, what did I want to do with my time?

As much as I thought I had sufficiently prepared beforehand by setting my own future goals and creating aspirations, I couldn't help but question my identity now that I was no longer a mother surrounded by her children.

What Defines Us

We are all well aware that motherhood is a job that requires a consistent focus on others besides ourselves. It's a given that, as we are raising our children, we moms take a hit when it comes to enjoying personal time. Any job that we are on call for 24/7 for 18 years and to which we readily respond—even when we're exhausted, at our wits' end, or down with the flu—involves some personal sacrifices.

But what happens . . .

- When the house is empty, and we *still* continue to let motherhood define who we are and what we do?

- When mothers continue to sacrifice themselves, their personal time, and their goals and dreams for their children, even *after* the nest is empty?

- When we think we've actually "let go" and don't even realize we're still controlled habitually by our motherhood identity?

- When we need to make a change to our daily life, and, more importantly, to our identity? And *why* even make one?

I often get asked about these concerns, because so many of us are overwhelmed when it comes to change, and rightly so. Even starting a positive life change has its challenges, and I'm surely no exception. Throughout my life—just like many others—I've struggled with questions about my identity. At different phases I've actively considered who I was, who I desired to be, and what I wanted from and in my life. To top this off, just when I felt I grasped some understanding of these matters, then life would throw me another curveball—usually a lesson of some kind that offered yet another opportunity to learn more about myself and humanity. While these lessons were not always easy, they did give me the opportunity to reconsider my prior answers and solutions.

While the questions and answers relating to our important concerns might change over time as our life situations change, and we are hit by yet another curveball, one thing remains consistent: *If our mindset is one that sees life's challenges as lessons rather than as mistakes or failures, there will be a healthy positive outcome.* That doesn't mean the challenges are any less frustrating—and it will still take time for us to be able to reap their benefits—but overall, the self-growth and awareness that can result make for a happier and more fulfilled life.

Many times I've upended my world and identity in the process of dealing with Lyme Disease, surviving domestic violence, relating to an ex-husband who was diagnosed as bipolar after we were married, stopping food addictions, simplifying my life, reducing everyday negativity, and so much more. At the time, all these journeys seemed life-changing and important (and still do). But if I had to pick one momentous, hard change that I'm proud about at this point in my life, it is my retirement from motherhood.

And I'm lovin' it!

A New Mindset

It happened when I was piecing some new goals together for myself eight months before our youngest, Chela, left home. Even though my kids weren't underfoot anymore on a daily basis in the house—they were grown up, and the older two had homes of their own already—I came to discover I wasn't able to focus on my own goals, because I *still* kept thinking about what the children would need, *even though they were highly capable of taking care of themselves at this point in time.* As I pondered and struggled to make some of my desired changes, a good friend of mine advised, "You know, moms *can* retire."

The words hit me like a punch to the gut, and momentarily dislocated my heart. Never in my life had I considered such inconceivable thoughts. I am a mother!

Initially I found the thought of retiring to be outrageous and nonsensical. I had dedicated my life to raising my children, and this had become my identity. So I truly questioned not only why I should, but also how I could, be "honorably discharged." And if I did "retire," was it possible to do so with morale and positivity—and without feeling like I was abandoning my loved ones? Maybe it wasn't what the kids themselves expected anymore, but I continued to feel that if I were to be a "good mom," I needed to be there at the drop of a hat.

And then there was the other side of the coin, with equally pressing and worrisome concerns, such as:

- How do I begin to live my own life, reinventing myself in some ways, yet remain connected to my adult children, especially if they no longer live with me, and if they have a job, or are off in professional school, and/or are serving in the military?

- Where do I fit in the scheme of their lives now? What's the fine line between supporting and codependent behavior?

- What are the rules that determine our roles and responsibilities now that the children are no longer kids, but are still our kids?

Once again, the concerns visited me late at night after the commotion of the day had subsided, leaving room for such worrisome questions. Sure, I always knew that one day, the time would come when my children would leave home.

But I never knew how I would move on too when it did.

One thing is for sure: There is no dodging change—it happens no matter what, and it's hard. But the good news is, there is a flip side to everything, if you look for it.

Living the Flip Side

To make this momentous change, and move on with my life, meant I had to reevaluate my perspective, reconsider my belief about the role of a "good mother," and figure out who I *was* and who I *could* be.

As I began to do this, opportunities turned into possibilities, and possibilities (along with some good ol' elbow grease and intention) evolved into realities.

Once I figured out who I was *besides* a mother, life opened up for me in countless ways.

No doubt you picked up this book and are either facing or experiencing the same, and in the following we'll explore how you can live life for you and still be a great mom.

PART I

PREPARING FOR THAT EMPTY NEST

Making a Smooth Transition

Chapter 1

HERE COME THE "LASTS"
Heart-wrenching Milestones

Motherhood has a way of interweaving growth and loss, from the moment the umbilical cord is physically cut to every milestone a child experiences and passes through. And those milestones are quite numerous. For a while the sleepless nights we spend nursing our crying babies seem endless, but before we know it, those babies of ours are crawling, walking, and running—and then it's the first day of kindergarten (another milestone!).

For two weeks prior to my son, Ishaan, starting kindergarten, I remember watching him proudly practice putting on his new "big boy" backpack. (It was blue, with a labyrinth of zippers and pockets.) For 20 minutes every day, he pretended he was waiting for the bus at the end of our driveway. I could hear him sing his own version of *The Wheels on the Bus*, between bites of apple slices. It was a sweet sight, yet my heart plummeted once Ishaan ventured out of my arms and into the schoolyard—a place where simply "anything" could happen to him.

Moms never know where life's adventures and experience will take our kids, but at that point in time, my son was entirely focused on his "big boy" school enterprise, and his excitement at starting a new adventure away from home—away from *me*—was my first uncomfortable dose of reality that kids do, whether their moms are ready or not, grow up one day.

I had to accept more changes when middle school rolled around, and my adoring child turned sassy and distant. I unhappily discovered the reality that kids at that age don't need or want their moms to coddle and pamper them much anymore. Indeed, I also often observed how many shrunk back in horror when their moms reached out a hand to show them some affection in front of their peers!

Middle school in particular is a time when we are often challenged with identifying the balance between setting boundaries and maintaining a two-way path of respect—all the while allowing our children to own newly constructed wings.

Here Come the "Lasts"

A blink of an eye later, the milestone of high school hits with intensity. Fortunately, it proves a time when moms can explore some mentorship and craft more of a friendship with their teens. For the adolescents, it's a period of self-discovery, dreams, mistakes, creations, and lessons. They truly no longer need the day-to-day kind of care their moms once gave them.

When my eldest son, James, left for the Air Force after graduating high school, Ishaan and Chela were eight and eleven years younger, respectively. So my husband Tony and I still felt like we had many years to go before an empty nest (and we did). While we hated seeing James's empty chair at the kitchen table, his leaving hit us differently than it would when our younger two were about to leave. It was five years later, when Ishaan was a junior and Tony and I attended a college night at his high school, that it hit me: Once Ishaan was not living at home, Tony and I would be left with only one child, and that daughter would be moving out a mere three years later.

So, although there had been many "lasts" I experienced with each childhood milestone, this period marked the beginning of even more heart-wrenching last episodes: Ishaan's last choir performance, his last playing-in-a-restaurant guitar gig, his last hike on Independence Trail, his last Future Farmers of America BBQ, his last school soccer game . . . and the last childhood birthday Ishaan would celebrate at home.

At each and every "last," I grew tearful.

I thought the experience might be a little easier on me by the time my third child, Chela, was getting ready to depart, and in a way, it was. After all, I knew I would survive it. But no one had prepared me for the "lasts" of my last child. I had three years with Chela as an "only" child, and in that time our relationship grew into a close friendship. We enjoyed our time together immeasurably and became so close that others often referred to us as "two peas in a pod!"

The first of these last episodes with Chela struck three months before her departure date, and I experienced emotional episodes nonstop from that point on: The last writing retreat together in Calistoga, the last picnic using our favorite blanket on the lawn, the last midterm written at my desk, the last community college graduation, the last book powwow at our favorite breakfast restaurant, the last night Chela would sleep in her childhood bed.

Then, finally, there was the last hug before she drove out of the driveway, leaving behind the nest I had built over 20-plus years ago. *Leaving* me *behind.*

Release Because They're Ready

With each of my children there were always more lasts. And guess what? Every single one, with every single one of my children, made my heart twinge. Although my pride in their independence and achievements is overwhelming, knowing that the children they were will never return has made for many weepy nights hugging my pillow.

Although it felt like it at times, I wasn't becoming hypersensitive or emotionally possessed; all of it was part of a natural and healthy transition. These feelings helped me prepare mentally and emotionally (one last at a time) for my child's upcoming flight. Such last episodes and the resulting twinges of the heart are a common experience in the process of moms letting their children go and grow.

When we actively resist such change, it's because we're still holding on to what the universe is asking us to release. Or, more simply, what *our children* are asking us to release: themselves. So we need to be wary of not allowing them to go and grow. Why? Well, over the years our children have become quite adept at reading our hearts. If we are having too much trouble letting go of our adult children, we are conveying to them that we think they *need* our help—which they will translate into our lack of confidence in their readiness to handle life on their own.

And that is exactly the opposite of how we want them to feel!

Chapter 2

A FRESH PERSPECTIVE
Doing What's Right for Your Kid

Spending time with our children as they grow up is a gift, and one I enshrine with gratitude. Yet, with work, school, meetings, extracurricular activities, housework, and the other inevitable realities of life, there isn't always a lot of quality time left over to spend with our children. Families are busy these days (*seriously, how many places can you be at once?*) but investing in regular quality time with our children can result in them generally feeling more secure, confident, and more cooperative.

We moms should make the most out of the couple of years we still have left with them while they are living at home, even if this means we need to kick ourselves into gear to do so! However, it also doesn't mean we have to go out of our way in a huge manner; the simple things are often the most effective.

Sit down for dinner with your children so you can have family conversations. Go out with them for walks after dinner and use the time to share some life lessons. The quality of the family time spent together (and not the quantity) is what will help turn conflict into connection, giving your young adult a happier and more stable entry to adulthood.

Now, this doesn't mean you should follow your teen around in high school and try to do everything with them. (That would surely drive them crazy and place a wedge between the two of you.) No, to successfully connect with them while they are still in high school, *you need to take a step back and see them for who they really are now*—and not who they are in your mind's eye. Indeed they have changed, even if they are still sporting that cute brown freckle they had on their cheek when they were born!

Throughout their life, your child has been developing a sense of self, identity, and self-awareness. Your growing child will have a whole new way of seeing themselves, as well as a new perspective as to how they view and need you. Yes, it sounds unsettling, but it's a natural and healthy adjustment, because something fundamental has to change in an adolescent for them to leave the safety and security of their home.

A Fresh Perspective

On a more scientific note, the baseline level of dopamine is lower in an adolescent's body than at any other time in their life. However, its release in response to experiences is higher. Dopamine is a chemical in the brain that is released when people engage with novelty, exercise, the unfamiliar, and the uncertain. This is a double-edged sword, for it generally makes an adolescent try riskier, sometimes dangerous, behaviors, yet at the same time it helps a child to feel more ready to leave home!

Just as an adolescent's perspective is changing, so should that of their parents. We moms are required to look at our growing children with a fresh perspective to help us better understand and respect their maturing identities. And to know who they are now, our high-school-aged children need freedom from our motherly grip to find themselves. Our children may be ready to take the next step toward adulthood, but we parents can actually hold them stagnant, in a needy or younger space, if we hold on to a limited perspective about what they can do for themselves, and to our long-held beliefs (which perhaps are no longer true or relevant) about who they are.

Treating an adolescent as a child can make them feel disempowered and humiliated. Of course they're still our kids, but they are at a very different stage of life now.

> **Too much coddling and overprotective-ness, and a mother's failure to acknowledge their growth, will prevent children, at any age from learning to feel and do for themselves, and to fly.**

When we continue to smother, pamper, aid, and abet our adolescents, whom are we really helping? Could it be we are satisfying our own need for purpose (*I'm a mom!*) at the expense of our child's individuality and growth?

I know taking a step back and looking at our grown children with a fresh perspective—*that they can do a lot of things quite well* without *our aid and interference*—is not easy because, for years, they have actively needed our care on a daily basis in countless ways. Our emotions and worries cause us to be so afraid of what we think *could happen* to our children if we don't continue to offer and exert the same assistance! Yet if we succumb to the influence of these emotions and concerns, we will continue to see them as fledglings rather than as the young adults they are.

> **So, as your child matures, rebuild a new relationship that is less about dependency and more about mutual respect, admiration, and a celebration of a budding, capable young adult.**

Rebuilding Your Relationship

Here are some ways to jumpstart that new perspective and begin rebuilding your relationship with your adolescent child:

- **Set boundaries for yourself, and practice giving your child space to grow.** Gracefully and gradually give up your front-and-center position in their lives. Learn to be quieter; give them fewer answers and ask more questions of them.

- **Give your child a chance to master tasks alone and learn from mistakes.** When your child makes a normal life mistake, instead of getting mad or frustrated at them, look at it as a teaching opportunity and a bonding opportunity.

- **Trust that the values you've instilled will inform their decisions.** Your child needs your trust to help them transition into adulthood. Trust is a gradual process that requires mutual commitment, and if you give it, it will inevitably strengthen your relationship with them. As a parent, you can't "demand" trust from them. Realize you just have to allow it to happen on its own merits over time.

Instead of picturing your child as a little bird whose wings may not hold them up when they take flight, take on a fresh perspective and *believe* in them . . . as fully capable of flying.

It's time to let your adult children spread, and use, their wings.

Chapter 3

LIFE OUTSIDE

Preparing Your Grown-up Kid for Success

No matter how accomplished we might be as individuals, isn't it also true that, according to our teens, we know "little" or "nothing" about the trials and tribulations of life?

In reality though, we do, because we're the ones *who are actually living those trials each and every day!* Truly, our adult kids can benefit from our experience and wisdom. So, despite my kids' initial resistance and "pooh-poohing" of my ideas, I still went about preparing them for their upcoming life as adults as best I could in these areas: domestically, emotionally, spiritually, and financially. I wanted to ensure my children were chock-full of knowledge and essential life skills before they left my household.

Here are four practical steps that you can use to help your grown child in the same way and prepare them to live outside the nest:

Step 1: Share Your WikiMom

Before a child moves out, moms have the ability to pass on basic life skills that are essential. If you know your child is leaving within a year or so, this is a great time to share with them (if you haven't already) how to care for themselves when they are living on their own. This sharing can and should include:

- domestic and maintenance skills

- financial skills

- academic and work skills

- social and emotional skills

- spiritual skills

- personal relationship skills

- self-care skills

- time-management skills

Domestic and Maintenance Skills

Do they know how to cook a meal? Have they ever done their laundry? Do they know what to hand wash, what to toss in the dryer, and what to line dry? Do they know how to check if a fire alarm is working, or what to do if they smell a gas leak? Do they know the difference between a flat-head and a Phillips-head screwdriver? Can they assemble basic possessions, such as a new desk or TV stand? Have they ever cleaned a bathroom? (And yes, by this, I mean the toilet!) Do they know how often to put the scrub brush in, and what supplies to use?

Financial Skills

Do they know how much money they have, and how to access it? Have they ever read a bank statement and maintained a simple budget? Do they know how to understand credit card, debit card, and loan offers? Do they know how to save for emergencies, and how to build a positive credit history without racking up debt? Do they know how much money they will need to earn monthly to survive on their own?

Academic and Work Skills

Have they developed basic skills in information and digital literacy, problem solving, critical thinking, and communication? Have they learned and demonstrated good work ethic traits such as reliability/dependability, dedication, productivity, cooperation, integrity, and a sense of responsibility? Do they understand the importance of placing an emphasis on quality, discipline, teamwork, and determination?

Social and Emotional Skills

Can they identify their emotions, and exhibit some self-control? Do they know how to wait patiently, solve problems, and delay gratification? Do they know how to set and achieve positive goals, and to feel and show empathy for others in order to establish and maintain positive relationships?

Spiritual Skills

Do they feel a sense of purpose and a connection to a greater observance? (Spiritual practice is deeply personal, and whatever your or their practice, it should nurture the soul.) Do they regularly work toward the greater good and help others who are in need of assistance? Do they take time to reflect on their life, and acknowledge how fortunate we all are for family, friends, and opportunities?

Personal Relationship Skills

Do they know how to say "no" if they're uncomfortable with or in a situation? Do they know the warning signs of an abusive relationship? Are they willing and able to voice emotions in an honest and mature way? Are they willing to apologize? (Everyone makes mistakes. Saying you're sorry and meaning it can go a long way after a fight.) Do they have basic sexual and birth-control knowledge?

Self-care Skills

Do they exhibit good personal hygiene? Do they get enough sleep and exercise regularly? Do they know simple nutrition and how to give their body the fuel it needs? Are they capable of giving someone their medical history? Do they know how to self-diagnose simple illnesses, and use a thermometer?

Time-management Skills

Do they know how to create a daily, weekly, and monthly to-do list? Do they know how to recognize procrastination, and to act instead of worry? Do they know how to effectively prioritize tasks based on importance and urgency?

<u>Putting It All Together</u>

While surely some of these skills will improve only with time and practice, it's still a good idea to talk them through so our children have a better understanding—plus, as their moms, we can rest assured thereafter that they won't starve to death or wear the same pair of underwear three weeks in a row when they're on their own.

I have often met mothers who didn't want their child to grow up helping around the house because "the child should play, not work, while they still can," "they should enjoy their childhood," or "I (*the mom*) should do all the chores because it's my job!"

Truthfully, there is no harm in giving a child responsibilities and teaching them how to help take care of the environment in which they are living. Doing so teaches them respect, responsibility, resourcefulness, and other essential life skills.

So, as their mother, think about what everyday living skills you would like your children to have when they live on their own, along with what skills will be important for their physical, emotional, and spiritual survival in this often crazy and hectic world of ours . . . and start as early as possible.

The truth is, you began preparing your child for independence from the beginning, when you helped them learn to speak and adhere to rules. But as your child grew into a teen or preteen, you may have stopped thinking about the specific lessons they needed to learn before leaving the nest. Become proactive by being attentive to those lessons now, and start on them as soon as possible, to give them time to gel.

For example, it's important for young adults to understand time management and the value of being on time, in order to become successful adults in life. Your kids need to understand that being late is actually a selfish act, because in using "one more minute" to do something, they're taking one more minute away from someone else. Arriving late to work or class is like saying, "I don't care about you or your schedule." Not a good way to represent themselves or build relationships, professional *and* personal. Being punctual also builds and reveals our self-discipline. It indicates that we honor our commitments and can be trusted to be reliable. It melts away unnecessary stresses and improves relationships. So, be attentive to teaching your adolescent children essential life skills while they're still in high school.

Be especially sure to give your children room to make mistakes while they still live

at home under your supervision. After all, it's probably the best place of all for them to learn.

So, don't yell at them or punish them if they shrink something in the dryer or use the Clorox to clean the hardwood floors. Keep it in perspective—and a bit of humor always helps, particularly if they catch their hair on fire while cooking pancakes. (Yes, that really happened to my Chela, and OMG, the smell of burning hair, ugh!)

Something I also want to mention: In our haste to avoid ever more disputes with our teenager, we may be apt to let chores or tasks slide. It's tough to handle conflict when we're tired or overworked, or have an overzealous debate-queen teen or sullen video-gaming teen. It's especially true if they're being resistant or downright unfriendly, giving us the eyeroll or hasty excuses in their desire to avoid real work. This, after all, will likely be the case if they haven't been doing chores like this since they were a child, right? It's not routine, so they will undoubtedly object, because they're going to want to hang out with their friends instead or go to see that cool movie. But . . .

We need to stick to our guns and remember all this is helping to prepare our teen for living on their own.

You may not get a "thank you" in the moment; more than likely, you'll receive a snicker or growl. But that "thank you" will come later—with their successful independence.

Step 2: Let Them Think for Themselves

Try to advise your adult child without pushing them. Do this by asking questions . . . *and being ready to listen and respond without judgment.*

Often when we ask a question, we have a preconceived idea of how we want our teen to answer. But part of allowing our children to grow up is recognizing that they are going to have their own ideas and own thoughts. Let them think for themselves. If you disagree with their answers and opinions, it's okay to let your alternative thought be known. But do so without pushing *your* way on them.

Step 3: Set the Framework for Independent Living and Expenses

Talk with your child well ahead of time (before "The Big Move-Out"), setting or establishing a framework for living on their own *now* so it's clear when they can ask for help (financially, emotionally, or otherwise) and when they will need to problem-solve by themselves.

Your young adult needs to know:

- How long can I live at home after graduating high school? If I can live at home for a while and choose to do so, will I have to pay you rent?

- Will you pay for all, part, or none of my tuition if I go to college?

- Will you help me out with my room and board? If I'm working, will you help me with the rent for an apartment?

- Are you going to pay for a meal plan while I'm at college, or am I responsible for buying my food?

- Are you going to pay my monthly cell phone charges, or is that on my shoulders?

- Will you get me a car, or am I supposed to buy that for myself? If I have to travel to college and don't have a car, will you help out with transportation charges (if I take a bus, train, or carpool)?

- If I have a car, who will pay the insurance, oil change charges, and gas?

Yes, it is time to share what the reality will be, so they are clear about what they need to do to make a successful move.

My husband and I told our children (while they were in middle school) that they would be financially responsible for their own college tuition, except for their book fees, which we would supply. While the kids didn't exactly jump up and down at this news, they knew the plan from an early age, and they accepted and understood that they had to save money if they wanted to attend college.

This news started the creation of bounteous lemonade stands held at the end of our driveway. It went from them selling just cups of lemonade, to selling homemade brownies, cookies, canned jellies, random garden veggies, and wildflower bouquets as well. (A quickly diminishing supply of my homemade canned goods soon led to an important discussion with the kids on gross and net profits!)

Then, approximately a year before each of our children moved out (so, when they were in high school), my husband and I sat down with them to make a categorized list of future living expenses. After we covered the entire spectrum—housing, food, clothing, medical, entertainment, etc.—with Chela, she was quiet for a time. Then she said slowly, "Oh . . . okay. Looks like I better get a second job before I move out." And she *did!* She taught herself web design and made a small business out of it, while also waitressing. In addition to this, she went about earning her black belt, dancing, and getting straight As at school. She was able to save enough money to move out successfully on her own, as well as to pay her own rent, food, and college tuition fees (with the help of scholarships that she spent countless hours researching and applying for)—just like her older brother had done three years earlier.

Now, sometimes it may look overwhelming and intimidating to a child when they see and understand the financial reality of their future—to the point where it feels impossible to manage. This is when your "momma power" can and should step in.

If your adult child is daunted by the realities ahead of them, research and learn *with* your adult child how they can make their future a doable reality. Please notice I wrote "*with*" them, and not *for* them. It's important they invest time and energy into what they want too, or else how will they even know if it really *is* what they want?

So, for example: Explain to them how they can look into scholarships and financial-aid packages, and also give them suggestions on how they can be budget-conscious. When considering household items they will need, suggest that they check local thrift stores or ask for hand-me-downs.

Six months before her departure, Chela wrote down a list of the household items she would need, and we had fun over the next six months collecting those items. She enjoyed my interest, and it helped make the move a reality once her moving boxes began to fill up. It also made me feel good to be a part of the process.

So, when it's about time, encourage your own young adult to compile a list of what they will need (like those household items). Also, help them create a financial plan so they understand their financial budget and how much they will need to work to reach it.

Where there is a will, there is a way.

Today, immediate gratification and a sense of entitlement are on the rise. We live in a world where the pleasure of the moment is much more alluring than the temporary impatience that is felt while in the pursuit of goals. We can get food in a matter of minutes from the drive-through, communicate instantly with texting, and have movies at our fingertips with Netflix.

Yet quick fixes that may satisfy us in the moment often leave us feeling unfulfilled and wanting more.

Our children and young adults live in this kind of world (just as we do). If they're under the age of 20, they've never known a world other than one that's on-demand. In our consumer-driven society, instant gratification is even *celebrated*. As a result, many children and young adults end up with the expectation that they will have what they want without any effort or responsibility on their part.

Getting caught in the gratification trap means you have an expectation to gain something from nothing—but the world doesn't work like that. We need to give something to get something back.

Start teaching your children how to be patient, to respect and learn a strong work ethic, and to see the value in putting forth effort—lots of it—to get the results they want. Being patient and working toward what we want helps build the resilience to face challenges, to not take things for granted, to problem-solve, to exhibit self-control, and to face the future with a vision.

Still to this day, my husband and I may hear a snide remark or see a reaction of disbelief regarding our children paying for their own college tuition. Maybe our framework isn't right for everyone, but it worked well for our family. Our children grew up with self-motivation and the belief that they can achieve what they work toward. This self-knowledge has lasted far beyond the lemonade stands and has enriched our children's adult lives. Our oldest, James, is a helicopter pilot, spending much of his time navigating the skies flying Euro-Copters (EC-130) and A-Stars. He's also a dedicated husband, and a father to sweet Emberly. Ishaan graduated magna cum laude, and is an actor and singer/songwriter in Hollywood. And our youngest, Chela, is currently studying screenwriting and linguistics—and her first fiction book is soon to be released.

The better your adult child knows themselves (the more prepared, confident, and self-aware they are), the easier it will be for them to determine a career path that is correct for them, beyond all of the obvious skill-set and educational requirements. And, if they are happy with what they do in life, they're more likely to be happy and successful overall.

I can vouch that seeing my adult children happy (in whatever personalized way that means to them) makes *me* feel happy and successful as a mom.

Step 4: Enjoy the Adventure

It's time to accept that your child is moving out. Be enthusiastic for them, and let your adult child know that you support them, love them, and are willing to be of help to them. (This is *so* much more constructive than fretting and worrying about them.) See their big move-out as an adventure and remember that long-ago time when *you* first moved out. Maybe it was scary, or exciting, or both—but whatever it was, it *was* an adventure, a life experience, and a momentous time of learning and growth.

While your son or daughter will always be your child, moving out marks the first steps of their independence. This is an exciting time for them, as they transition from child to adult.

If your child is frightened at the prospect of leaving, it's important to reassure them by telling them that the unknown is worse than the reality. Help them to understand that a parent wants their child to stand on their own, and it gives you pleasure to witness this. Remind them that once they're into their new routine, it'll become fun, familiar (it'll become their "comfort zone" soon enough), and they'll be successful.

Then, listen to your own advice, *and walk your talk by remembering to acknowledge your own feelings too.* As your adult child becomes independent, your life will rapidly change. Your own apprehensive feelings, such as questioning your identity or purpose, may suddenly become overwhelming and intensified.

Let's explore that in more depth.

Chapter 4

WHAT ARE *YOUR* NEEDS?
The Change Affects You Too

Many of us moms have a hard time letting go of our kids when they first move out because it has become our identity and habit to take care of others, and our children in particular. Our newly empty nests force us to reevaluate our lives and to look at our own selves too.

This can be hard, even scary, because we don't always like what we see. Sometimes how we think we're living life and how we *actually* live life are two different things, and this becomes more apparent when we slow down—like when the house is suddenly empty and the mirrors plentiful.

When all the busyness of helping our child get situated wears off, we will start to notice there's been a big change in our own life. Well, change is good, *and* change is hard, *and* change happens. It is that very inevitability that makes change predictable and disrupts our equilibrium.

Life is a dynamic balance of negatives and positives, and focusing on the positive aspects of change can be the difference between growing and thriving in any environment or experiencing continuing sadness.

If we begin to look to and consider our own needs *before* our children actually leave, setting up a framework for new life goals *of our own*, we have a better chance of rebounding with a happy life after they go, and finding joy in those new opportunities that will lie before us. Planning ahead is always best, but it's not too late to start today to look at your own needs for the first time in a while.

When one chapter of our lives is completed and closes, it's time to start another.

We will never stop loving and supporting our adult children, even when they are no longer under our roofs, but our active parenting role does change, and so it's a good time to focus attention on our own needs and goals.

Ready, Set, Aim

It's time to take action. Not only will it feel good, but it's inspiring to our children if they see us working toward something. Children of all ages—even those living on their own—relish seeing their parents build a life that doesn't revolve completely around them. It takes some pressure off both mom and child, and it also gives us moms guilt-free permission to do the things we've put off for months (or, in my case, decades).

Perhaps you have some personal goals already in mind. If not, think about *possibilities* . . . What will inspire *you?* Maybe it's taking up a new hobby or talent, starting a new career, or building new friendships. Maybe it's a focus on better health, learning pottery, writing poetry, going back to school, or traveling the world. Whatever it is you want to do—begin to do it!

The best way to start is *by taking that first step*—just like your child did so many years ago when they felt the potent desire to walk. Just as you encouraged your child to try walking and influenced your children over the years to try new things and follow their dreams and goals, it's time to encourage yourself with the same compassion and support.

The Looking Glass

As moms, we must come to accept that our children are grown now and capable. We also must recognize that *doing so makes us look squarely at our own selves.* And with no one left at home, it can feel like the bathroom mirror suddenly quadruples in size.

Without a doubt, we begin looking at our own magnified reflection, and it becomes common to question the past, the present, and the future. Without the distraction of the kids, we are left staring in the mirror, reflecting on whom we did or didn't become during the child-rearing years—and often questioning if we did or didn't do enough.

So, what's *your* first step?

Start by making a list of all the things you've been putting off and pin it somewhere where you'll see it often. Don't forget to add novel things you've never thought of doing before, but that now seem attractive or inspiring to you. Then mark off the items on the list as you achieve them one by one.

If you do this, you'll revive your interests and passions, while reinventing your life . . . and yourself!

PART II

LET THEM FLY

Reinventing Your Relationship with Them (and You) Once They Move Out

Chapter 5

THE BIG CRY
Expect Some Tears in the Silence

Rarely does anything about mothering ever happen in a predictable way or as we imagine it—including the "Big Move-Out."

I knew it would be hard when my kids headed off to college. I just never knew it would be *this* hard. So I cried. Not just a sprinkling of dewdrops, but wracking, heart-clenching sobs with each and every child who left. I gave myself permission to cry, but the ferocity of my tears (especially when my daughter, the last of my children, left) surprised even me. Yes, my tears fell, one by one hitting the kitchen table as I sat surrounded by a silence so sharp it stabbed at the maternal instinct so ingrained in me to love and protect my children.

Where had the time gone? I wondered. I thought about how sleepless nights nursing and cuddling a baby at home had turned into sleepless nights worrying about a teenager out for the evening doing who-knows-what.

All the time-outs had transitioned into move-outs! All I could think was, what am I going to do without the laughter, the friendship, the daily communications, and the sharing of meals together?

When I finally managed to stop the ferocious flood of tears, I could practically hear in the silence of my kitchen my heartbeat echoing throughout the empty house. My husband comforted me with hugs; he knew it would take time for me to adjust to this change.

While Tony was affected emotionally by our children's departures, it just wasn't in the same way. Over the years, I had been the primary one at home raising the children (although I did work teaching martial arts part-time), while Tony was at work, teaching full-time at our martial arts studio. Yet Tony has always had a graceful way of adjusting more quickly to change than me. So during the times when our children first left, he proved very supportive (and patient) with me. We shared some tears, hugs, and thoughtful conversation, but I also endured many quiet moments reflecting on the last 23 years of my life.

I was only 20 years old when Ishaan was born, so barely out of the teenage years myself. At the time, I was filled with dreams of being an actress, a veterinarian, or a naturopath. The world was full of possibilities and I had a passion inside me that I didn't fully understand, but that made me feel creative, inspired, and invincible.

Then, seemingly in the blink of an eye, I was 43 years old and 50 pounds heavier. I was sporting fine wrinkles and feeling alone. Actually, even more than feeling alone, I felt *shocked*, like a deer caught in the headlights. After 23 years of a life filled with children, I had to watch as the last one pulled out of the driveway one sunny morning, knowing that afterward, my life would never, ever again be the same. Yes, that was a shock! Even though I knew so many years earlier while I cradled my baby in my arms that one day Chela would be moving out, it didn't make the change any easier.

I missed the little things the most. Making funny faces at each other and bursting into laughter. Our spontaneous vegan cooking extravaganzas (although, I don't think my meat-and-potato-loving husband missed this much). Seeing the new contraptions James would build and watching him skateboard in front of the house. Hearing Ishaan's guitar strumming and Chela's piano tunes float through the house. The spontaneous living-room dance shows Chela would entertain me with, and sitting down together to watch the TV series *Chicago Fire* after a long day. Their beautiful voices when they sang, and the calling out of "Mom!" from down the hallway. Eating smoothies on the deck together and soaking up the sun. I even missed seeing dirty clothes on the bedroom floor and tousled bed covers.

But I really, really missed our heart-to-heart conversations.

I was left in shock. *Who am I?* I wondered. If I'm not going to wipe away their tears, drive them where they need to go, prepare their meals, and engage in lengthy conversations with them about a variety of topics, then . . . how will I fill my time?

I had been defined as a mother for 23 years, so this change in identity would take some getting used to. My job as a mother was no longer a daily, attending-to-their-needs job. I was going to have to wait for their phone calls, and realize that when I called or FaceTimed, sometimes there would be no answer.

It's Time

All moms, at some time or another, have to let their children grow up and go. Naturally, the passage of time is a big help in processing this new life change.

We all want our kids to become independent, happy, thriving young adults, but even so, there is a twinge of grief that comes with letting them go. When our children become adults, we will grow and evolve too, but as with any change, doing so can be uncomfortable at first.

Be easy on yourself, and remember it is normal to feel sad and cry a little.

I don't think moms can avoid experiencing this pain, this loss, regardless of how prepared we think we are for our children to step across another threshold. So it's okay to cry upon their departure. It's not even *selfish* to cry.

As you mourn the loss of your kids' daily presence in your home, please understand you won't be recorded in the *Guinness Book of World Records* as "World's Loneliest Mom" (even if you qualify as an honorable mention). And your crying won't make you any less valuable, or less worthwhile, as a person. So go ahead: *Let it out.* It's better than keeping it locked inside until some trigger unlocks it at the worst time imaginable, and your tears explode like Mount St. Helens once did, spewing emotional ash on anyone within a 100-mile radius.

But also remember we moms are all different. So, some of us may cry more deeply than others, others may cry for longer periods of time than others, and still others may simply cry louder than others. The intensity of our tears might be different too, if the leaving of our children happens to coincide with another big event in our lives (which is quite common). We may find it more difficult to cope, for example, with our child moving out if we are also undergoing menopause or an illness.

> Note
>
> If this is the case for you, keep an eye on those tears. If you cry excessively for weeks on end, or you start to feel your life has no meaning, or you feel isolated and find it hard to spend time with your friends, your grief might have turned into something more serious. If you find that you're not coping and feel a deep sense of emptiness or depression, or an inability to get your life back on track after the children leave, it's important to receive professional help.

No matter what depths of grief you may feel, or how many or few tears you cry, take care of yourself. Pamper yourself. Treat yourself to a massage, go on a hike, read a good book, buy an outfit, or indulge in a favorite meal or treat. Do something nice for yourself while grieving, because all sadness and no happy moments is a surefire recipe for depression.

Acknowledge the Grief

To deal with letting go of their child-turned-adult and letting go of their active role as a mother, some moms find it extremely helpful to have a letting-go therapeutic ritual.

For example, you might plant a tree, light a candle, and/or share memories with others about your child. You might make a scrapbook for your adult child, including baby photos and special mama moments (my adult son loved this, and still today enjoys looking through the memories), or light a Japanese lantern and let it float down the river. Just about anything goes because the change is personal to you, and there is no right or wrong way to process change.

But most important is to acknowledge your grief and let it move through your system. Resist the temptation to compare yourself to other mothers going through the same thing. We are all different, and we will process change in our own time and in our own way.

As for me, eventually I got to the truth: All moms, at some time or another, have to let their children grow up and go.

Chapter 6

A QUESTION OF CONTROL
Striking a Healthy Balance

The question I hear asked time and time again, especially from mothers of newly relocated adult children, is this: "Where is the fine line between healthy and unhealthy control?" Control, or having a "sense of control," is a deep-seated need all of us desire to fulfill.

When we first become parents, it makes sense to exert a healthy degree of control over our children because they are unfamiliar with the ways of the world. So we usually choose to control situations with our young children through the use of boundaries. Boundaries are about both understanding and respecting our own needs, and being respectful and understanding of the needs of others. For example, we may teach our kids such boundaries as "no hitting," "don't interrupt," and "knock before entering the bedroom." Young children generally benefit from this use of boundaries, as the practice makes it easier for them to understand what acceptable behavior is and what it is not.

When Ishaan was four years old, I once took him to preschool naked. For the past week, he had put up a struggle whenever I tried to get him dressed for the day. On this particular day, he refused to put on any clothes, and despite my efforts, tore them off within seconds. So, I buckled him into his car seat and drove him to preschool naked. I walked him up the steps and through the door—bare buns and all. He was met by many curious pairs of eyes staring at him—and when he realized everyone else was dressed, he immediately wanted his clothes on.

Ishaan never put up a fuss about getting dressed again, and that's because learning boundaries helps children to self-regulate their own internal dialogue and produce healthy guidelines for themselves. However, everyone likes some degree of control, even children. As our children learn to navigate the world, figure out their role in life, and learn just what they have power over, they're going to want to show us *they* are in control. So after our children's initial years, it's usually advisable to gradually let our kids take some control of their own selves as they grow and progress through middle school and high school.

A Question of Control

Still, despite us moms knowing intellectually and rationally that there's value in releasing some control, doing so often proves hard to accept and implement. Our children's assertion of control often means their refusal to listen to us or follow our directions, and this can be difficult for parents to navigate and accept.

As mothers we may begin to feel a sense of loss of control as our child progresses through the developmental stages, but this is especially evident upon the big move-out—especially if we didn't plan ahead and start letting our children do things for themselves earlier on in their lives. For if we didn't loosen our grip on the reins of parental control as our kids grew up, we are likely to find it especially tough to do so when faced with an empty nest.

This happened to one mom I interviewed. Maggie couldn't let go, even once her son Jon moved six hours away. She would call him and suggest things like, "You're doing so well with the social media business you started, I think you'd be better off, and do great, as a businessman in the corporate world." But Maggie knew full well that Jon loved working with his creativity and had work a nine-to-five corporate job like his father.

For Maggie, the loss of daily control in her child's life was difficult to accept, something that can be true for most moms. Why? Our nest has turned helter-skelter, and our adult child no longer needs us and the same kind of maternal involvement in their lives as they once did. As we struggle to come to terms with this, we may still find ourselves saying or texting certain things to them to try and "nonchalantly" sway our children's decisions to fit *our* ideals or standards.

All in all, it's just not easy to stop wanting to control our kids' lives even when they are no longer living under our own roof. That desire will sneak up on us again, and again, and again.

Letting Go of the Reins

We need to remember, *it's not about us.*

So before you tell your adult child you will help fill out their job application because they don't have a computer, think again. Is it because you really want them to have this job and you'd feel better if they did? *Probably.* Is it because you like feeling needed? *Probably.*

"But she doesn't have a computer," you say, "so I have to help."

Not true. That's a poor excuse. The truth is, you still want to be Wonder Mom who saves the day (for your own benefit—you will feel needed by your kids if you do), and you also are trying to keep your adult child from taking on responsibility.

In this day and age, Moms, computers are widely available. If your daughter truly wants this job, she will find a way to get the application and submit it. As a result, she will be more invested in the application process, which in turn creates confidence and leads to attainable success.

A better option than doing it for your child (and definitely a less controlling one) is to tell your adult child you are happy to look at the application with them, or you're available if they have any questions about it—then let it go. *This lets her know you care and support her without trying to control the situation.*

What about if your son calls and needs to borrow money to make his rent that month? You know it's tight and he's been working hard, but you also know that last week he bought a $200 pair of boots. *Do you step in and help?*

Sure you'll want to dig out your "Wonder Mom" cape and save the day, but sometimes having it a little hard helps a person put their priorities into perspective. Maybe in this case, it would have proved more beneficial for your son to have waited before purchasing those expensive boots and to have applied the available money to his rent instead.

When you don't support each beck and call from your kids, it gives them an opportunity to learn a lesson from their mistakes—just as we did (and still do). Of course it's hard, because no mom likes to see their child suffer. I personally had a hard time letting go at first, because I was so close to my children when they lived at home. They talked about everything with me, from the best place to get gas, to their budding relationships, to their dreams and passions. The feeling of disconnect after they moved out was one of the hardest adjustments for me. However, what you need to do is:

Trust in your children and their process.

If they are struggling, and you see a quick fix or a positive way out, naturally you want to help. But it's good to remember this is *their* life now. *It's time for them to make their own choices and their own memories.*

So, as situations arise with your adult child, how do you know whether to take a step back and let them figure it out on their own, or to help them?

Stop. Look. Listen.

When your adult child raises an issue with you, before you act or react, use the "stop, look, listen" technique. This is a simple three-second method that you can use to question yourself before you give a response or answer. I learned to use this defense mechanism in my Frequency Energy Medicine™ studies with Dr. Ondre Seltzer. It's powerful because it's about sensing and reacting, and *it gives you a few seconds to make a decision.* Stop, look, listen can be used in all areas of life (such as when quick decision making is needed, for personal safety, for self-awareness, and in relationships). In the realms of motherhood the technique gives you enough time to reground yourself.

- **Stop** means you stop whatever you're doing in that moment. This gives you time to quickly clear your mind, so you can approach a situation with a calm mind.

- **Look** at the whole picture (for example, don't focus on the fact that your daughter is crying on the phone or your son is complaining about working too much), so that you can figure out, what do they really need? (Is it money? No, not usually.)

- **Listen**—not just with your ears to hear your child's verbal utterances and responses, but also pay attention to what you are feeling. What are you feeling on the inside, and also, what are you feeling from your son or daughter? For example, are they taking advantage of you? Are you feeling disrespected? Or do you feel loved and cared for? Are you feeling a heart connection?

Once you stop, look, listen (remember, this only takes three seconds!), you can respond to your child's request from a grounded and more centered self. You'll find that using this method heightens your self-awareness, and it can also be used as a personal-safety technique (for example, if you find yourself in the wrong part of town, you can use the stop, look, listen method, and *act* with logic and intuition rather than *reacting* with "panic.)"

Stop, look, listen can also be used in any situation that might catch you by surprise—and one thing moms can count on is being caught off-guard at one time or another. For 55-year-old Barbara, this was the case when her son called to ask if he could borrow $40,000 to avoid bankruptcy. She was caught off-guard and immediately said she would help him. Then she practiced stop, look, listen and, five seconds later, said to Nate, "Actually, I don't have that kind of money and this is your responsibility. You got yourself into it, and it's time to get yourself out. You're a grown man now."

A week later when Barbara told me her response, she said it still hurt her heart to administer this type of tough love. Money was no problem for Barbara and many times in the past she had forked out money. But after she practiced stop, look, listen, she became more aware and knew, in the long run, that it wouldn't help her son to lend him money. Nate had to live this lesson and face the situation at hand by taking responsibility. She had to learn to stop, look, listen to obtain a full, well-rounded perspective as to what was going on.

Their Growth and Well-being

So in the future, when your adult child asks you for assistance—be it practical, emotional, financial, or otherwise—and the worrisome thought intrudes, *I've been helping them all their life; how do I know when to continue helping them, and when to step back?*

Stop, look, listen.

Then, before you utter a word in response, ask yourself: Is the response I am going to give going to fulfill a need to stay involved and in charge of their life, or is it smarter for me, in this particular instance, to take a step back and offer up a response that focuses instead on the well-being and growth of my adult child?

Look very, very closely though, because it's easy to justify just about anything when it comes to helping our children.

Rest assured, they will always be your children. You will always be their mom. So it's okay to step back, shake off some control, and trust in *their* process.

Chapter 7

THE NO-WIN CYCLE
Guilt, Perfectionism, Judgment, Control

Moms are famous for feeling guilty. Even the most proficient and loving of moms can have feelings of inadequacy and of not being enough, or doing enough, or of not doing the right thing for their children. We may wonder if the choices we've made for our children throughout their lives will have any lasting negative effects—and if different choices would have made for happier, more well-adjusted adult children.

Guilt is an emotion that makes us think. And, as with all emotions, guilt can drive us—or it can destroy us. It can help us figure out how to make things feel right, or it can eat away at our self-worth when we feel we can't change a situation.

Whenever a mom can't live up to her own standards, she often falls into guilt. In other words, if she can't or doesn't make some things *right* for her kids (whether or not they live at home), she can at least feel like she is a good person because she feels guilty about it. And who's the biggest critic here? The person who judges us the most harshly?

We are.

The No-win Cycle

This guilt can create a no-win cycle in terms of our relationship with our adult kids, one impacted by control, perfectionism, judgment, and guilt. This cycle may start with you trying to *control* a situation with your adult child, perhaps trying too hard to make it *perfect* for them. When the outcome doesn't meet your own (perhaps, far-fetched or idealistic) standards you begin to *judge* and question your decisions and actions. This can make you feel *guilty* and inadequate in a variety of ways (the ways differ from person to person). This then diminishes your self-belief, and your sense of your own value as a person and as a mom.

> **If you are lacking in self-belief, you will be left shieldless in a battle against feelings of unworthiness and guilt.**

This is what happened to Janet. When her daughter Alexa was in her second year of college, Janet started pushing Alexa to get a job. She did this by constantly initiating the job hunt for her daughter. Finally, and as a direct result of her mother's relentless involvement in the situation, Alexa ended up getting a part-time job as a waitress at Denny's. However, the job required Alexa to work some very late hours, and this resulted in Janet worrying about her daughter's safety (the job she helped her child get wasn't the *perfect* one in terms of its hours). And indeed, one night, Alexa was mugged while walking from work to her car. Immediately, Janet began experiencing extreme guilt over pressuring her child into taking a job in the first place.

Guilt poured into Janet like an open floodgate, and she began questioning and judging her own actions and intelligence. The mind chatter started: *I never should have pushed her into a job. This never would have happened if I'd just stayed quiet. What was I thinking? It was stupid of me to push Alexa into taking a job that required working a night shift!"*

Janet now felt completely guilty—and was faced with the reality that she was not in control of Alexa's life. In order to maintain her desired level of control, Janet started encouraging Alexa to call and complain (to make Janet feel needed) and sending her extra money (because she felt awful about the mugging). Janet's reaction then prompted the same kind of guilt-inducing cycle to reboot again.

And again.

Breaking the No-win Cycle

Often, even despite our best efforts to be different, we get up each morning and find ourselves thinking, behaving, and feeling the same way we did yesterday—and the days, months, and years before that. *Why?*

Perhaps it's because life has a funny way of teaching us lessons.

> **When there is something we need to learn, something that we need to work on, the same situation will continue to repeat itself until we either find a healthy way of dealing with that particular issue or learn our lesson.**

Indeed, the key to breaking any cycle of negativity (for example, the desire to control someone else's life, a need for motherly perfectionism, an addiction to smoking, poor eating habits, and so on) is *to shift our state of mind and alter our current perspective.* Unfortunately, this shift doesn't happen overnight, especially because habits become hard to break;

they are deeply wired into our brains by their constant repetition.

But by becoming conscious of our negative habit(s) and focusing on our desired goal to reach a new healthy habit, we can change the way we think, and thus, the way we act and/or react in given situations.

Steps to Break the Cycle

The following three-step practice can help you to identify any triggers and create a new goal by reframing how you are going to act, then use perseverance to create a healthier new behavior.

Step 1: Identify Any Triggers

In the beginning, your goal isn't to *judge* yourself or feel *guilty* about doing something unhealthy or unproductive. The goal is to be *aware* of when and why it happens. For example, when you eat, is it because you are hungry, or is it fulfilling a feeling inside you that needs to be comforted? (If you are feeling a lack of control within a situation, the act of controlling what you put in your mouth can temporarily mask your discomfort.) Or, when you pick up your phone, is it to contact someone, or are you grabbing it to distract yourself from a task at hand by scrolling endlessly on Instagram or browsing Facebook to see the latest post?

Trying to ignore the behavior you want to change might seem like a good way to vanquish it, but in fact, it's exactly the opposite. To break a bad pattern, you'll need to *increase* your awareness of what you're doing in the first place, and what it was that gave rise to it.

Step 2: Frame New Goal(s)

It's easy to approach a habit you want to change by saying, "I'm *not* going to eat sweets anymore," or "I'm *not* going to call my daughter three times a day." But here, you're focusing on what you're *not* going to do.

Instead, *put the focus on the goal itself,* such as, "I'm going to have a piece of fruit every time I want a sweet," or, "I'm going to turn my cell phone off for part of the day," or, "I'm going to set a boundary." When you tune into those "permission-giving" thoughts and look at them critically, you're better able to call yourself out and hold yourself accountable when the urge to engage in your bad habit strikes again.

Step 3: Don't Give Up

Breaking bad habits takes time and effort, but mostly *perseverance.* Realize that it will take time for the new brain connections to kick in, for the old brain firings to calm down, and for all the new patterns to replace the old. So don't beat yourself up for slip-ups or use them as excuses for quitting.

> **No one is *perfect.* Motherhood is not for wimps—and it's not made to be a perfect flight either.**

Focus on being great—the best *you* can be—instead of being perfect. Allow yourself the room to make mistakes.

Put Away the Perfectionist

Speaking of being perfect: *How do you know if you're expecting too much of yourself?* Some telltale signs of perfectionism are:

- setting impossibly high standards
- being overly eager to please others
- being highly critical of others
- being quick to judge others or yourself
- holding on to a specific manner in which things should be done

- possessing a "go-big-or-go-home" attitude

- allowing little or no room for mistakes

- exhibiting grumpiness if something doesn't go the way you've planned

Perfectionism is a double-edged sword because it's driven by our well-meaning desire to do well, and by a fear of the consequences of not doing well. The fear of failure (and the resulting procrastination) is the perfectionist's nemesis. Although perfectionism is characterized by an intense drive to succeed, *it's also what stops us dead in our tracks!*

If the conditions are not perfect or they can't see a perfect outcome, the perfectionist may never start. They want things to be completely perfect from the get-go, and will only start when they feel in control—which usually happens only when they have all their ducks in a row and everything is organized to their standards. But this rarely happens because in the mind of perfectionist, things could always be better—*somehow.*

Once our children move out, it's crucial to begin focusing less on trying to be perfect or on controlling every part of our children's lives and to stop feeling guilty about the results if we do (or even if we don't). Staying in a mindset where a desire for perfection (or the need for control) rules our thoughts and actions is likely to create unnecessary emotional turbulence for ourselves—as in Heidi's case.

Heidi was a good mom. She loved her children and always put them first, even to her own detriment. When Zac, her youngest son, moved out, she wanted everything to be perfect. Secretly she prided herself on feeling in control of the big move-out and his life thereafter. She contacted Zac often, and genuinely wanted to be involved in what he was doing.

It was not until Zac had a girlfriend in college that he emotionally pulled away from his mom a little. But Heidi, being so used to having an active involvement in Zac's life, wasn't aware of her son's new need for space—both physically (in terms of fewer phone calls and less input about his life) and emotionally (Zac needed space to think and feel his own thoughts). Because Heidi was so focused on maintaining her standards, she wasn't aware of Zac's crucial growth change. What could have been a smooth transition turned into a huge pull-away by Zac. He rarely called his mother anymore, and when he did, he didn't want to hear any suggestions Heidi might have.

The change stung. Mom and son had always been so close—often sharing ideas, jokes, stories, and laughter—so when Zac first pulled away, Heidi felt like she had failed at being a good mom. Her desire to be the "perfect mother" bit her in the heart with a sting that hurt beyond words.

Three painful months passed before Heidi realized that she had been so focused on being a perfect parent that she had failed to be aware of what her son really needed once he moved out: love and support with space to think and feel for himself.

If Control Is Your Issue

What if you just can't seem to stop putting in your two cents about how things *should be* in your children's lives now that they've moved out? What if you just can't seem to ever trust in *their* process?

Have you stopped to consider that maybe *your need* to control every aspect of your children's lives even when they no longer live under your roof might not have anything to do with them?

Maybe it's all about you, Mom!

If we have developed what has become an unhealthy need to control, we need to face our feelings and reach an understanding of where they generated from. Coming from a place of logic and intuition:

• promotes a deeper understanding

- inaugurates a healthy sense of control

- reduces our tendency toward impulsive, emotionally charged actions and reactions

When we reach and maintain a place of healthy control in a relationship, it is because the two people involved have developed a connection based on:

- mutual respect

- trust

- honesty

- separate identities

- support

- good communication

Of course, all of these things take practice. And the truth is, each relationship in our life—whether it be a friendship, workplace relationship, or relationship with family members—is most likely to be a combination of both healthy and unhealthy characteristics. For healthy control is not easy to find or maintain.

It takes unflinching self-awareness to see past our habits, worries, and insecurities to understand why we are feeling and acting the way we are in any given situation.

Of course, this all begs the question, *why do so many of us even end up feeling an unhealthy need to control?* Often it's because we are lacking in self-worth.

When Self-worth and Judgment Are in Play

Many of us allow outside factors to negatively influence our inner sense of value and self-worth. Factors such as:

- other people's actions, judgments, and reactions

- expectations from our loved ones

- job demands

- society's unspoken standards

- the rules written down on paper

In fact, everything *outside of our body* is an external source.

Take Lucille, for example. Lucille didn't feel valued as a person because her daughter didn't call her (her daughter's *action)* once she moved out of Lucille's nest. This made Lucille feel like she was losing her connection with, and control over, her 22-year-old. Lucille's reaction (which was both emotional and impulsive) was to turn to eating excess food to comfort her inability to control the upsetting situation.

The No-win Cycle

Lucille was exhibiting an unhealthy sense of control. Yes, Lucille was in control of the hand that was putting the cookies in her mouth, but this *reaction* was covering up the real issue. Lucille's real issue stemmed from her *low self-belief and self-worth.* Her internal chatter and belief went like this: *My daughter doesn't call me back when I ask, so this must mean she doesn't love me! Clearly, I wasn't a very good mother. Nobody likes me.* And in Lucille's case, when she didn't feel valued as a person (often triggered by her daughter not calling), she just ate more and more cookies. Doing so satisfied her desire to feel in control—even if it was a negative and unhealthy kind of control.

You see, when our need to control is *unhealthy* and *negative*, we feel a tension between our need for control and the evidence of our unhealthy control—which may reveal itself through such things as drug, alcohol, or food addiction—or through simply needing things a certain way. Unhealthy control can lead to passivity, fear of change, and letting other people or situations control us.

So we tread a risky path when we base our self-worth on external sources. We start to make our choices based on a desire to control outside situations and the people around us, which, ironically, only leads to an inadequate and negative sense of self-control and self-belief.

Letting Go

Although at first, it may feel like we're losing control when we let go of a situation, the opposite is at work. Sometimes letting go and trusting in the process is more powerful than trying to control. Another mother, Kirstan, fell into the trap of believing that if she could just do and say *all the right things*, then her relationship with her daughter Jayme (and with others) would be strong. She made it her job to try to do everything she could to make sure the people around her were always happy—and she did the same when she talked to Jayme on the phone. Kirstan learned the hard way that she couldn't control what others thought of her—or how they chose to experience life.

She reached this understanding soon after Jayme, who was working as a waitress in a restaurant, texted her one evening to say, "I quit my job tonight." Jayme's shocking statement was followed by a series of angry emoji faces.

Kirstan phoned Jayme immediately, and found out that her daughter had quit because Jayme's boss, who had been drunk, had started yelling and belittling her daughter.

Kirstan felt responsible for the mess because she felt it was her duty to make sure her daughter was always happy. She wanted to fix it for Jayme, and also to make her feel better. Without telling her plans to her daughter, Kirstan jumped in the car the next morning and drove five hours nonstop in order to see and console her daughter. But when she arrived at Jayme's place, she wasn't even there. Kirstan texted her daughter, and soon found out Jayme was with friends at a BBQ. When she got her mother's message, Jayme texted her mom back that she'd be home after the BBQ was over, in about three or four hours.

Obviously, Jayme wasn't too broken up over the restaurant fiasco. Clearly, she didn't need her mom to drive down to "fix" things. But Kirstan had driven there all because she wanted to control the situation and its outcome—without bothering to find out what her adult daughter truly needed.

As she waited for Jayme to arrive back, Kirstan realized Jayme was an adult who would do what she wanted to do, see what she wanted to see, hear what she wanted to hear, and act as she wanted to act—whether her mother was involved *or not*. From that day forward, Kirstan invested less time in trying to please her daughter and others. She listened and offered advice when her daughter asked—but she also stepped back and let Jayme feel her own emotions, and make her own decisions as a result, without her mother's constant input.

As a result of lacking self-worth, Kirstan chose to focus on everybody else's problems rather than her own. She focused on making everyone around her happy. Why? Like a Band-Aid, it temporarily masked her internal feelings of inadequacy that stemmed from low self-worth.

Kirstan learned to only be responsible for *her own actions and intentions*. She learned to focus more of her time and energy on living in a way that reflects *her* personal values instead of trying to control her daughter's perceptions. This means her self-worth took leaps and bounds forward. She is less stressed and much happier now that she has let go of the reins.

As we are able to acquire a healthy sense of control, we become *proactive* and *self-motivated*. Internally, through our strong sense of self-belief, we gain the ability to control our habits or addictions. This helps us approach situations from a place of self-worth and strengthens our ability to influence the world around us in a positive and healthy way. But how do we begin? How do we build up our self-worth and self-esteem, so that we can build a healthy relationship with ourselves and our adult children?

We will discuss this in more detail in Part III. For the time being, the important takeaway here is that we can learn to value ourselves by taking responsibility for our own happiness, instead of basing it on external measures.

Chapter 8

HELLO, WORRYWART!
Allowing for Risks, Responsibility, and Capability

Motherhood, no matter what chapter we're on, brings out the worrywart in all of us. From the day we bring our sons or daughters home, we are hardwired to protect those kids. The worrying starts when they're young, when we moms have to be responsible for so much of their life: their safety, their health, their burgeoning social skills, their education. So we worry they're going to slip or fall on the playground or we fret that they may not look both ways when they cross the street.

Then, when they become adolescents, we worry about different things:

- Did they study for the test last night?

- Are they going to make their curfew?

- How hot-and-heavy is date night out going to be? Are they being careful?

- Are there any chaperones at the party they're attending? Will there be alcohol or drugs on the premises?

Off they go to college, and the worrying continues. We can't help but wonder (a.k.a., *worry*) about things like:

- Are they eating well?

- Are they studying enough, and turning in assignments on time?

- Are they making healthy choices?

- Are they budgeting their funds?

- Are they making friends with people who are going to be a good influence on them?

Or, if they move out on their own and are working full-time, we worry about:

- Are they going to hear the alarm?

- Are they being punctual and arriving at work on time?

- Are they meeting deadlines?

- Are they getting along with their colleagues and roommates, and impressing their supervisor?

Also, we worry about issues that are specific to their own individual situations, especially if our adult children have a high-risk sort of job or live in an unhealthy environment.

I remember the specific moment my oldest son, James, called to tell me that his buddy had been in a helicopter crash earlier that day. Of course I knew my own son faced this same potential danger every day, but upon hearing the news, I could hardly breathe. (And to this day, my heart jumps into my throat if the phone rings at an odd hour.)

Letting go of worrying so our grown children can thrive unencumbered by our anxieties is the ultimate parental challenge.

Amy struggled with this very thing. Currently she has two grown daughters: Ellen is in college, and Megan is working and lives five hours away. Well, Amy not only had a knack for worrying, but also felt if she *didn't* worry, she wasn't being a caring mom *(uh-oh . . . guilt alert!)*. Even when Amy's daughters were doing well, she created situations to worry about. She would call and find something big or small to awaken her worry bug.

If Megan mentioned that she wasn't sure if she would be able to take a trip abroad that year because she "didn't have the money budgeted for it," Amy would pounce, discussing finances so much that Megan would become worried that she wasn't making enough money, and would never be able to save up enough, with her current job.

Or, when speaking to Ellen, Amy would bring up her daughter's college boyfriend in a condescending way. She would ask how many hours Daniel was working on the side, and if that effort was enough to survive on his own and take her out on dates. She even said Daniel's psychology major could be potentially harmful to the couple's relationship because Daniel would "always be assessing Ellen's actions."

Amy riled up both her daughters so much that they became worried about issues in their life that they were handling fine beforehand.

This story is similar to that of Catherine, a Facebook mom who checked on both her daughters' pages countless times a day. She constantly "liked" and responded to their posts with lengthy comments. Essentially, Catherine wanted to be a good mom, but that translated as interfering with her daughters' ability to live their own lives.

In contrast, Denise put her son Carson on her Find Your Friends app when he moved several states away. In this way, Denise could check up on him and see where he was, but she didn't constantly call him or get in touch; she let him live his life and initiate the contact between them on his own terms.

Having Carson on her app was reassuring to Denise. If something bad happened and she didn't hear from him for several days or a week, she could track him from a distance in terms of his cell phone location to set her mind at ease without actively intruding on his life. And if Carson was to call and inform her that he was stranded somewhere, she could easily alert the police to his whereabouts because she could see where he was stuck.

Finding a Happy Medium

We are always reckoning with how we can find a happy medium in raising our kids: allowing them enough experience and risk to foster the development of the kind of competence, confidence, and courage they'll need to become well-rounded, flourishing adults, while still prioritizing their safety and well-being.

If our kids are coddled for too long, they run to mom to fix it when they make mistakes, and they don't learn to deal with the repercussions or consequences of their actions for themselves. Ultimately this doesn't teach them responsibility. Plus, our children don't feel like they are capable of addressing whatever it is in front of them that requires their attention.

This was the cycle between Amy and her children—and it existed long before her daughters actually took flight. By the time the girls moved out, they were already dependent on their mom as the go-to Wonder Mom who would solve any of their problems—be it a social altercation, work dispute, or anxiety attack.

Amy hadn't realized the profound negative effect that her Wonder Mom role would have on her daughters (she thought she was being helpful!). But *her* worry inspired *their* worry, thus constructing a negative cycle based on fulfilling Amy's emotional desire to feel needed.

So, the next time you open your mouth to speak on the phone with your child, please do your best to remember that while a little worrying might pass as an expression of love and caring, too much worry can be selfish and detrimental to the parent–adult child relationship.

The reality is that worry quite often ends up being a *selfish* act. When we worry about our children, we end up focusing on our kids' problems rather than dealing with our own.

Too often, we worry because we have a need to feel needed. (As you have already read, we moms feel good when we're "needed.") But what have we created if this is a constant when our children are living on their own?

Have you ever heard the phrase, "I'll scratch your back if you scratch mine?" This idea of helping someone to get some help in return is the essence of a symbiotic relationship. It's based on a relationship of *dependence*. Additionally, worrying is detrimental to our very selves, because it:

- causes stress

- robs us of energy

- masks other emotions that need our attention (like guilt, perfectionism, and control)

Keeping Your Lips Zipped

I've said it before, and I'll say it again: *Overprotecting our kids doesn't help; it hinders.* We are supposed to make mistakes and learn from them during our lives. Taking healthy risks and making mistakes is a natural element in understanding how the world works and comprehending what our physical and emotional boundaries are. After all, it only takes one touch on a burning hot stove to learn we can get burned—and to never do it again.

So the next time you're about to air your worries to your child, remind yourself that the last thing you want is to make your grown children feel insecure and teach them that they aren't capable after all—or cause them to become irritated with you. Because if they become annoyed with you, they're less likely to stay in touch, and then you'll have no idea what's going on with them and in their lives.

And the one thing I know *all* of us moms of grown kids want is to hear from the kids once they've moved out.

Chapter 9

ONE WORD THAT MAKES ALL THE DIFFERENCE
Avoiding the Guilt Trap

Allowing a child to grow into an adult without feelings of guilt is essential for their future well-being. In particular, the common practice of guilt-tripping our adult children about how much they *should* call us or visit us really won't encourage them to do either. In other words, it backfires.

Just ask Justine, who worked guilt tactics to get the results she wanted from her children before they had even left her nest. For example, she would make her daughter Rachel feel guilty in high school if she went out with a friend instead of having a popcorn movie night at home with her mom. Justine would say in a condescending way, "Do you *really* have to go out tonight?" or "You always spend time with your friends—but remember, *I* won't be around forever!"

Justine continued this routine of trying to make her daughter feel guilty even once she was away in college. She made Rachel feel overwhelmed with guilt over not checking in with her mother each and every day. The outcome of this guilt-tripping was that Justine and her daughter had little to no communication for several years after she first moved out. Only at holidays did Justine's daughter bite the bullet and give her mom a quick call.

A Neat Trick

Happily, I've come to discover a quick fix that can help your relationship with your adult child to last, and the communication between the two of you to thrive. What's more, it's pretty easy, actually:

> **If there's a "but" in the sentence you're about to use with your adult child, think again before actually using it.**

Usually a "but" contrasts with something that has already been said. For example, if you say, "I know you are really busy, *but* I want to spend time with you," you aren't truly acknowledging or appreciating their busy life. "But" is a conjunction that is used to marry two contrasting ideas and in this case, often leads to the guilt factor. Instead, try replacing "but" with "and." Try this on for size: "I know you are busy, *and* I want to spend more time with you."

Do you see how this simple change acknowledges your child's busy life while also sharing your feelings? This approach is better suited to finding a solution rather than causing agitation, anger, or guilt. Here are some more examples:

- "You did great on your science paper, but what about your English essay?" The "but" lends a doubtful tone and leaves an emotional space to fill. Try saying, "You did great on your science paper, and what about your English essay?" The "and" opens up communication, whereas the "but" shuts it down.

- "Your girlfriend is nice, but she's shy." The "but" turns this statement into more of a judgment. Try saying, "Your girlfriend is nice and I noticed she is shy." This releases any sense of judgment and makes it a non-threatening observation.

- "I agree with a lot of what you're saying, but I wonder if we can look at this point further?" Using "but" in this sentence devalues the person's thoughts or ideas. Instead, try saying, "I agree with a lot of what you're saying, and I wonder if we can look at this point further?" This gives value to the person and the conversation without you trying to control it.

And, in the case of apologies:

- I'm sorry you feel that way, but_____.
- I'm sorry my words hurt you, but_____.
- I'm sorry for what I did, but_____.

With apologies, it's best to leave the apology on its own: "I'm sorry you feel that way." "I'm sorry my words hurt you." "I'm sorry for what I did." And that's because the word "but" negates the apology. What it's saying is, "I feel compelled socially to apologize, but deep down I believe I am right, and you are wrong." In apologies, critiques, and in other complex communication, "but" is often an impediment in these sensitive situations.

Be aware of your words. Simply removing the "but" and replacing it with "and" can improve the quality, and the extent and frequency, of the communication between you and your adult child.

The good news is, this happened with Justine! She adopted this practice, *and* it's taking time, *and* slowly Justine is gaining her daughter's respect back through respecting her as an adult and understanding that she has new friends and a new life. Do the same.

Give your child the space to live their life now.

We really shouldn't mind if they like to do activities with their friends and without us. We have our own lives and they have theirs. Be sensitive to your child's need to grow, experience, and become their own person. And be sensitive to your need to do the same. You might be surprised at the very pleasant outcome.

Chapter 10

STAYING IN TOUCH
Ways to Communicate

In the "old days" (okay, when I was growing up), it was more difficult to communicate with family members who lived a long distance away. After attending Sierra College (50 minutes from Nevada City), I moved out of state with my boyfriend to Ashland, Oregon. This was a big deal for me at the time, as most of my large extended family were located in Grass Valley, California. Ashland is only six hours away, but it might as well have been across the country. Months would pass without talking to the cousins I grew up with. Once a week, I would break down and call my parents and siblings—then I'd have to deal with the expensive long-distance charges. Mail (yes, snail mail) was one of my favorite means of communication because I enjoyed writing, and better yet, I enjoyed checking the mailbox in hopes of a letter from home. (Old-fashioned or not, I still love to write letters! James, Ishaan, and Chela find a note in their mailbox every couple of months these days.)

Since my mom couldn't just physically turn around and tell me things like she used to or pick up the phone and reach me instantly, because the phone she was calling might be out of hearing distance—and I didn't even have a message machine back then—a sense of loneliness, distance, disconnection, and alienation developed sometimes . . . in her, and definitely even in me. So yes, keeping up communication with your child is vital in maintaining family togetherness and in keeping up to date with any news.

Today, parents are fortunate to have many resources available that allow them to stay connected with their children. With a simple touch of our thumbs or a word into the microphone, we can text and reach our loved ones instantly. In the "old days" we had to dial a rotary phone in the hopes someone would answer. (On Amazon.com, if you like, you can buy a retro rotary landline phone . . . retro. They're commonly found in mustard yellow or petrol blue. Am I really that old?)

Of course, social media has made communication easier. With one click, we can share our news with our followers, and help us keep up with existing friends and reconnect with old ones. From what you had for dinner that night to your child's graduation, it's easy for all to see what's happening in your life. Gone are the days of printing and mailing photos to Aunt Mabel. Now uploading and sharing vibrant photographs to family and friends is only ever a click away. Social media creates a bridge with family, friends, and events that, because of time and geographic constraints, you wouldn't otherwise see and learn about.

Video chat is another great modern boon, as it is (almost) as good as being able to sit down face-to-face and chat in the living room together. The gestures we make, the way we sit, how fast we talk, how close we stand, how much eye contact we make—even when we're silent and just listening as the other person talks, we're sending messages. Being able to see the person you are talking with not only enhances the conversation, but also eliminates the frustrations of not being able to see all the non-verbal communication that you miss on the phone.

I remember the first time I used FaceTime. It was Ishaan's 20th birthday. He was in Los Angeles and I was 446 miles away at home, and not being able to spend his birthday with him was just about killing me. Then, happily, we FaceTimed, and I watched as he opened the small gift we had sent to him in the mail. From our home, Chela, Tony, and I then sang him "Happy Birthday" while he listened, watched, and grinned from ear to ear. Being able to share an event with your family takes on a whole new meaning when you can see and hear your loved ones.

I also use Skype and Zoom—both video chat apps—for my business once a week when I teach online workshops. Friends and family can use it to keep connected, too. Skype technology requires Wi-Fi or 3G service to run, and guess what? Within the USA it's free communication! Also, Skype Credit's per-minute rates for calling internationally are cheaper than other options. Since we have it, it allows us to never think twice about calling up our relatives in Germany.

A Double-edged Sword

Now, although there are many ways of communicating with our children, I need to add a line that you'll have heard before: **Proceed with caution.**

At first, we may want to check in with our children six times a day to find out what they're eating for breakfast, lunch, and dinner. We call to ask if they turned the lights off to save on electricity, and we simply must check in to make sure they arrived home safely from work, or to remind them it's Uncle John's birthday today. However, as much as we moms *want* to call or text, try and refrain from contacting your children *too* often.

In this digital age, the real risk is that parents will remain in charge of directing their adult child's every move, no matter where in the country they attend college or work a job.

Instant messaging, e-mail, and cell phones allow for immediate contact, and this is the real double-edged sword. For college-age children, the journey toward independence will be short-circuited if their parents continue to micromanage their lives.

In those "old days" I remember it was common for parents to drop their college students off at college and tell them to "call home once a week" as they waved goodbye and hollered, "See you at winter break!" Today, however, it's extraordinarily easy for parents to interfere in a college student's new life with a quick call, a short email, or a simple text.

Sheri recently shared with me that she schedules a weekly phone call with her moved-out son to say hi and catch up. This gives her son space, and by the time a week passes, there are fun things for them to share, making for a quality conversation. Sheri explained that when she used to contact Gregg once a day, the interactions were short and lacked substance, and often ended on an agitated note.

When my Chela first left home (after a long, heartfelt hug!), she jumped into her Ford Focus (the red "doodle-bug," we called it), which was loaded with her clothes, bedding, dishes, toilet paper, and much more. And, just like that, she was out the driveway and gone. Tony picked up the phone to call her after 15 minutes. But, as much as I also wanted to talk to her for the entire 446.5 miles she drove to LA, he and I decided together to put the phone down and instead, spend the time as she drove to her new abode reminiscing about all our happy memories of Chela growing up. (OMG! They grow up so fast!)

It's easy to want to be involved, and it's fun because they are young and adventurous and that touches our adventure button, and perhaps reminds us of a time in our own life that felt free and full of possibility. But it's their turn now for their own adventure, as it is our turn to start our new adventure without kids.

If, in our daily lives, we moms are cell-phone fanatics or accomplished trigger-happy texters, we rarely give our adult children a chance to practice independence. It's practically like they never left home, and it leaves them little space to spread those wings.

I have a couple of friends who are horrified when I tell them that I sent Ishaan off to Washington, D.C., with a small group of middle-school kids and a couple of school teachers when he was 11 years old. It's actually pretty common, but for many the thought is still a resounding, "I'd never let my middle-school child do that." Was it easy? Honestly, I fretted a bit, but I did it anyway because I knew how important this would be to his overall growth and confidence.

Chela was 16 when she traveled to Germany by herself. She eventually met up with Fenna, her German friend, but not before flying 11.5 hours and navigating parts of Frankfurt by herself. As a self-defense instructor, I am fully aware of all the statistics. (For example, females aged 16 to 24 years old are four times more likely to be sexually assaulted than women in other age groups. And in the United States alone, one violent crime is committed every 18 seconds, and one forcible rape every four minutes). So thoughts such as these are always fresh in my mind. But . . .

Sometimes you have to trust in something higher and believe in your child's ability.

The self-growth that developed from that initial solo trip changed Chela forever, making her feel mature and capable on a mental and emotional level. The other side effects from that new experience of independence for Chela were that she took an interest in foreign languages, and went on to learn German, Spanish, and French too. Independence is self-belief you can't achieve if you rely on your mom (or anyone else). Importantly, it's where "the magic happens"— where inspiration develops, and dreams and goals are born.

It seems it's usually best, for parents and children alike, if we begin the pull back sooner, even when a child takes that first step into a kindergarten classroom. Balanced involvement and guidance without dictating on the parents' part helps our children to make their own decisions. By the time college rolls around, we will all be less dependent on each other and more ready to make progress independently with respect, encouragement, and the space to go in our own directions.

Chapter 11

A WALK IN THEIR SHOES
Building a Lasting Relationship with Your Adult Child

When James left home to join the Air Force, they didn't require him to bring much in the way of material items, so he only took a few belongings. He packed his bag with a few clothes, a toothbrush, an extra pair of boots, and his iPhone.

James was excited about this change in his life, even though his stomach was in knots; he truly did not know what to expect. I understood his uneasy anticipation, because I remember the nervous feeling I had when I moved from my childhood home (where I had spent 19 years making memories with my family, including raising dairy goats, learning how to garden, and making applesauce with my mom) to live in a studio apartment by myself. Tony related to James' mix of emotions even more deeply than me, because he too had joined the military and also experienced similar feelings of anticipation—especially in regard to the commitment that would dictate the direction of the next four years of his life.

> **Empathy, or the ability to understand and share another's feelings, plays a big part in building lasting relationships with our adult children (and in any relationship).**

With empathy, we vicariously experience what another is feeling, as if it were our own emotion. When we are *empathetic*, we are stepping into a person's shoes and co-experiencing the world from their perspective or through their eyes. Through empathy we can relate to others' emotional or situational realities more readily. Empathy is easily confused with *sympathy*. However, with sympathy, we acknowledge the other person's feelings, but we don't really *feel* what they are feeling—it's more of a knowing.

Healthy Doses of Empathy

Healthy doses of empathy help build and improve relationships with our adult children in these three ways:

Dose #1: Patience and Understanding

Many times, we can lose our temper and immediately fall into an emotional response when we hear about something our adult child is going through, like declining a promotion or changing majors. Empathy, however, forces us to step into our child's shoes *and see things from their perspective.* Even if we sport different opinions or tastes from our grown children, we can learn to appreciate and respect their views if we empathize with them.

For example, when Veronica's son, Eli, graduated from college with his teaching degree, everyone expected him to accept the high school teaching position that was offered to him. Eli, however, had different plans. He decided to travel in Europe for the next year before settling down in a job. At first, Veronica admitted that she felt disappointed, even angry, at his decision to decline a job and forfeit a consistent salary. But after Eli enthusiastically shared his plans to see the Eiffel Tower in Paris, the Trevi Fountain in Rome, and Buckingham Palace in London, Veronica felt empathy—feeling his joy and enthusiasm *as if it were her own.* And it was then that she became okay with, and excited by, Eli's decision.

Dose #2: It's Not All About Me

When we empathize with our adult children, we can see our own emotional motives more easily, and we also can see why they may get annoyed at us for the ways we handle certain things. A healthy sense of empathy, partnered with a bit of open communication and a good laugh, builds quality, lasting relationships.

Nate had been living on his own for three years when he had a small falling-out with his mom, Hannah. He was changing jobs, and his life was pretty much up in the air. For a period of two months, whenever he called home, the conversation was full of his complaints: "I don't have enough money," "Nobody is respecting my work," "The traffic is terrible," and "I hate living in San Francisco." Nate thought only about himself during these conversations, and never asked anything about his mom and her life.

Hannah, being the resourceful mom that she is, started to give him advice. This resulted in a flood of anger from Nate, as he was in a self-pity mode and didn't want to be "fixed," as he termed it. Even though Hannah perceived his problems to be mostly a common-sense, easy fix with an attitude change or simple actions, she realized it didn't matter what she said. At this point in Nate's life, he had lessons of his own to learn and he wasn't going to listen—

yet he still needed to know that his mom loved and supported him. Hannah changed her approach from trying to "fix" the situation to simply listening to Nate without judgment or agenda. And she didn't wait for him to ask about her day. She openly shared about what was going on in her life, and this took some focus off Nate. It wasn't until Hannah empathized with Nate that they could hold conversations to keep connected without Nate feeling angry, and without Hannah feeling his emotions "dumped" upon herself.

Dose #3: Paying Attention to How Our Actions Affect Others

This is crucial if we wish to maintain a healthy relationship with our adult children. When we are empathetic, we can begin to understand if we are smothering our kids, or conversely, not giving them enough attention. Hurtful actions and comments can stay in people's memories for years, so it's imperative that we cultivate emotional intelligence. Everything we do and say to people has an effect on them—and we never know to what extent.

For example, I remember running in for dinner once when I was eight years old, and my mom, dad, older brother, and sister were already sitting at the table and engaged in conversation. Although I was a good six years younger than my siblings, I wanted to put my two cents in, too, so I shared what I thought about vegetarianism. But I pronounced the word wrong, and it came out mangled—making it sound funny to my entire family. They all turned to face me in the kitchen where I innocently stood . . . and laughed. (I know they weren't trying to make me feel bad, but terrible is how I felt.) I developed a fear of being judged and laughed at, and it wasn't until after high school that I began to feel comfortable speaking my thoughts out loud again. Even today, I sometimes stutter when saying words that are difficult to pronounce.

The Other Side of the Coin

Yet . . . *everything in moderation.* While empathy is important to cultivate in the relationship with our adult child, it's also true that having too much empathy does not always end up being a positive. Read on to discover how too much empathy—*or overdoing the feeling of another person's feelings*—can actually create a toxic relationship with your child.

Chapter 12

WHOSE PROBLEMS ARE THEY REALLY?

Overdosing on Empathy

One weekend, Chela and I were in the same room on a weekend girls-only writing retreat. As writing often goes, it takes time, patience, and perseverance. My daughter and I experienced many uplifting and positive hours there, but we also both had our fair share of frustration and downright discouragement at points. At one point, my inner self-chatter sounded something like, *Why would anyone want to read what I just wrote? OMG, this makes no sense at all!*

However, during a time when I was feeling quite good about my flow of words and ideas, I heard my daughter on the other side of the room let out a frustrated sigh. Being empathetic, I immediately could feel her frustration, and so I flashed her an understanding smile before continuing on with my own work.

Only a minute or two later, I began to struggle with my own writing. Frustrated, I rested my chin in my left hand and stared aimlessly at the words in front of me. My creative flow had suddenly been cut short. I had been on a roll, so why was I now stalled and irked?

That's when I saw it: I looked across the room to the table where my daughter was writing, only to realize I had not only taken on her emotions, but was also physically mirroring her, down to my chin being supported by my left hand, my slightly slumped posture, and my furrowed forehead. This time, the emotion of frustration and writer's block wasn't mine; I was feeling my daughter's angst, and it had short-circuited my own writing flow and mood.

How often does this happen to us as mothers? How often are we unaware that an emotion we feel is often not even ours but that of our child—yet we claim it?

It's something you might do with your own child, especially once they are off on their own and you are listening to them express frustration over the phone or via a text. Think about it: Have you ever gotten off the phone after talking with your child, and then suddenly felt stressed and in a bad mood? Could it be because of what they are experiencing at the time? *Absolutely.*

And it can sneak up on you. During your conversation with them, everything might feel okay, but a few minutes after you get off the phone, the emotion can hit you like a ton of bricks!

Recognizing Empathy Overload

When we have *too much* empathy for our adult child (or another person), we may experience "toxic energy" and feel one or more of the following[*]:

- fatigue or exhaustion

- copycat symptoms

- unusual health conditions

- certain physical symptoms only around certain people

- tightness or constriction in the solar plexus or upper chest

- strange eye or vision issues (blurry eyes or seeing spots)

---

[*]Full credit for this list of symptoms is given to Dr. Ondre Seltzer, Ph.D., Frequency Energy Medicine™.

- sudden drop in energy

- different tastes and smells

- depression or sadness

- "seeing red," or experiencing "dark" energy

- inability to focus

- paranoia and anxiety

- heightened or unusual fears

- unusual dreams

- apathy

A Symbiotic Relationship

So, the next time you begin to feel something that seems out of the blue or is a case of strange timing, take the time to stop, look, listen (see Chapter 6 for a refresher). Pay close attention: *Maybe you are picking up on another's (your child's?) emotion that's not truly yours.*

If we live without an awareness of what is going on, our care and empathy for our kids can develop into a harmful symbiotic relationship with them. Unhealthy empathy, or "symbiotic empathy" (as referred to in Frequency Energy Medicine™), is when another person's problems, such as our child's, become our own.

Whose Problems are They Really?

When we take on our child's negative emotional energy *as ours*, we start carrying this toxic energy around with us, and it can contaminate everything, including the rest of our family, our friends, and even our pets. We all are made up of energy, and so we have an energy exchange—one that can be either positive or negative—with every single person with whom we interact.

As moms, we want to help our children with so much fervor and passion. But it is when we identify *too much* with what they are feeling, and our desire to help them becomes a bit unhinged, that it becomes unhealthy for them—and for us.

Yes, that's right! Symbiotic empathy functions like an umbilical cord.

The toxic energy goes both ways. We have to be careful that we don't take their negative energy on, and also that we don't put too much out.

It's easy and more common than you'd think for moms to find themselves in the web of a *symbiotic empathy relationship* with their adult children. Fortunately, the stop, look, listen technique can effectively help us increase our awareness and avoid unnecessary toxic energy.

When worrywart Kirstan (from Chapter 7) understood the effect that her unhealthy worry and empathetic reaction was having on her adult children (she was making her daughters emotionally codependent), she was, with some professional help, able to identify her habit, then make a change.

The change happened by Kirstan first understanding her own habits and dependency. She had an addiction to feeling needed by her kids, which stemmed from her not having a strong sense of self-worth. With help, she was able to change her negative codependency relationship with her daughters. She started transforming their unhealthy symbiotic empathy relationship into a healthy relationship between adults—one that was based on self-value and compassion. By doing this, among other things, she slowly started to gain the self-belief that gave her the freedom to make guilt-free choices based around her own dreams and goals.

Chapter 13

DID I DO ENOUGH?
Setting the Bar

When my children prepared to move out, I couldn't help but question myself with each child: Did I do enough to prepare them for the outside world? A world filled with Muggles and magicians, happiness and hate, success and stress, good people and bad people? Many of my friends asked this same question, too, and we all assured each other, "We did the best we could." But the mom who is a perfectionist (yep, I'm guilty of this one, and you can assess whether you're a perfectionist by a look at Chapter 7) will always find something big or small to pick at and say, "I could've done better here . . ."

> If you're a perfectionist mom—and even if you're not—relax and take a deep breath. At some point, yes, we all probably could have done better.

Frankly, it's tough to be a mom, mostly due to our perception of *how we want things to be*—and it's also impossible to be a perfect one.

Many of us have set the bar way too high for what we need to do to be the perfect mom—or even just a good one. Trying to keep up with the online Joneses, the Pinterest-worthy perfection posts, and the ginger-glazed-Mahi-Mahi-with-roasted-butternut-risotto Facebook dinner posts by the mother who has five well-groomed, high-achieving, and polite children is incredibly unrealistic. Plus, when we get caught up in how we think things *should be* and compare our lives to other people's, we are losing touch with the reality of what's really important—our health and happiness.

Let's not spend time any longer beating ourselves up with the *should haves* and *could haves*. What's done is done, and it's time to focus on the future. By the time our kids move out, they are young adults, and it is *their* responsibility to take care of themselves. Seriously, it's now time to cut that energetic umbilical cord (*again!*). No one is perfect, and it's okay to make mistakes (and to have made them in the past)—and that goes for your kids as well as yourself.

Enjoy the Journey

There is no perfect way to raise a child. And, as I've said before, sometimes the more "perfect" we try to make things, and the more we try to control every outcome, the more likely it becomes that the universe will throw a monkey wrench directly in the middle of our perfect plan. Did you ever stop to consider that if our kids' lives become too "perfect" and they always get what they want, they don't have healthy boundaries and consistency, they're not held accountable for their actions, and they don't learn?

And what is life really about?

Learning and self-growth.

Nature has a funny way of teaching us lessons, if we try too hard to make things perfect or control every outcome.

Remember, a mistake only stays a mistake if we don't learn from it; otherwise, it's a lesson. It's far less stressful, and more joyful and fun, for everyone to loosen up instead of being so worried and uptight about getting it "right."

PART III

LIVING LIFE FOR *YOU*

The Next Chapter

Chapter 14

INTO THE LOOKING GLASS
Focusing on Your Journey

Moms, it's time to begin focusing on *your journey* rather than *your child's destination*. It's time to start enjoying your life *right now* instead of focusing solely on the outcome of your children's adulthood and your value as a "good mom." Remember that too much focus on the outcome puts you in a headspace of idealism and teaches your children to respond to life with a similar attitude.

Instead of focusing your time and energy on worries, comparisons, self-judgments, and perfectionism; on trying to be "better than" or "as good as" everyone else; and on attempting to make your adult kids' lives perfect, why not focus on the best *you* can be now that you have some time for you . . . and enjoy yourself while you're at it? Of course, doing so makes us look squarely at our own selves. And with no one left at home, the bathroom mirror might seem like it has suddenly quadrupled in size.

Without a doubt, when we begin looking at our own magnified reflections, it is common for us to question our past, our present, and our future. Without the distraction of the kids, we are left staring in the mirror, reflecting on the person we did—or didn't—become during the child-rearing years. When we think about who we are, we might be shocked to discover that we are highly critical of our very selves, our lives' progress and journeys, and where we might be at this point in time. So many of us have low self-esteem, and that is not good for anyone!

It's time to look at *your* reflection in a different way. It is time to care about your value and accept your own self.

To jump-start the self-value and self-belief process—and help yourself let go of comparisons and judgments—you have to do three things:

- allow
- admit
- acknowledge

Allow

Allow compassion into your life and use it to love and understand yourself. Wikipedia states, "Self-compassion is extending compassion to one's self in instances of perceived inadequacy, failure, or general suffering." The significance of this wording lies in the term "perceived inadequacy" of self. That means it is not necessarily the truth that we are really inadequate!

As long as we have inner mind chatter that beats us up for our imperfections, we'll find ourselves caught in a negative storyline and will find it difficult to be compassionate to our own selves. The good news is that we all have a natural capacity for compassion; we just may have allowed life experiences, social pressures, and everyday stresses to suppress it. Yet self-compassion can help us change the behaviors that make us feel unhealthy or unhappy.

Having self-compassion is not an egotistical thing, and it does not involve self-pity. It simply allows for *personal well-being.*

Developing Self-compassion

The key to developing compassion is to have a daily practice, and the following two practices, used regularly, can help transform your relationship with yourself:

Self-Compassion Practice #1: Invest in Yourself

In order to offer compassion to others, we first must fulfill ourselves. If you are suffering, be kind to yourself. Treat yourself like you are your own best friend forever (your own BFF), or how you would treat your child.

Taking care of yourself to regain balance and well-being can be as simple as going for a daily 10-minute walk or taking a hot bubble bath. Maybe it's scheduling a pampered spa weekend away or a rejuvenating massage. I know this all sounds good, but surprisingly few of us actually do these things, because we moms are the best at coming up with every reason (excuses, really) why *not* to—because no matter what, we always have something to do for someone else, or have somewhere else to be. So ask yourself, do any of the following excuses sound familiar?

- "Sounds fun, but I should pay the bills today."
- "I can't—it's Jon's field trip and I'm chaperoning."
- "I've got to send these emails first."

- "Maybe I'll relax and read after I wash the dishes, do the laundry, and help the kids complete their homework."

Let's face it: *The list is never done!* Even when we have an empty nest, that damn list is still there. So get yourself off the *bottom* of your to-do list and put yourself *on top*. Do it by scheduling a few simple acts for yourself, every day, and just let the self-compassion trickle in.

Self-compassion Practice #2: Be Mindful

Mindful people feel what they are feeling. Being mindful doesn't imply feeling happy all the time: It is about *accepting* the moment we are in and feeling whatever it is we feel *without resisting or controlling it.* Sounds pretty simple, doesn't it? But when we start to pay attention to what we're actually paying attention to, we are likely to find that, most of the time, our minds are . . . all over the place.

Did you notice if you woke up tired this morning, if you greeted the day with a smile, or if the daffodils were in bloom? (*Yup, that's what I thought* . . .) Life gets busy, and we forget to check in with how we are feeling and what we *really need to be doing.* This makes it easy to get caught up in the stream of self-criticism that plagues our minds, with self-chatter such as:

- "I am so stupid."

- "I should have known better."

- "I'm a terrible mom."

- "I'm so fat."

- "Nobody likes me."

And on and on the relentlessly critical mind-chatter cycles, usually stuck on repeat.

> **Mindfulness is having nonjudgmental awareness that focuses our conscious awareness on the present moment. The present is constantly moving toward the future.**

Being mindful gives us space—space to breathe, space to think, and space between our emotions and our reactions. We can practice mindfulness as a daily habit, yet it is a lifelong process.

We are all made up of three components: mind, body, and spirit. All these three aspects need equal amounts of our care and attention. We feel happy, healthy, and motivated when we are balanced in *all* areas. When we focus too much on one area—even if it is a positive focus—the other aspects of our selves are likely to be unbalanced. For example, if we focus too much on work at the office, our bodies may lack the exercise they need, or we may not get out in nature enough to replenish our spirits. If we focus on exercise and nutrition without engaging our minds in learning, we may also become unbalanced.

Like mindfulness, balancing your mind, body, and spirit is a daily habit as well as a lifelong process. So don't expect it to happen overnight if one day you decide to be mindful. It takes daily practice and commitment. It's less about reaching a final destination, and more about being present and making choices that reflect what you want to achieve in a given moment.

The stop, look, listen three-second rule (see Chapter 6) is a crucial component in developing mindfulness: We can apply it to help us develop a heightened awareness in any situation. In fact, applying nonjudgmental awareness to our thoughts and reactions can help us see what is needed in order to develop self-compassion. Maybe it's as simple as getting out in nature. Spending time in nature is a sure way to reset our mental and spiritual states, and this directly helps harmonize the body.

Mindfulness and creativity also go hand-in-hand. So if your mind is stuck cycling on repeat, put on your creativity hat and paint, doodle, write a poem, bake, or sing in the shower. Notice how your mind quiets down when you do.

Mindful people are also conscious of what they put in their bodies. So often we are guilty of shoveling food in our mouths, without taking notice as to what we're even eating. Partial blame goes to society's quick pace (and all those on-the-run fast foods that are available to us 24/7)—but it really comes down to a choice. *Our* choice.

Mindful people make a practice of listening to their bodies and make a conscious effort to be aware of what they put in them.

Just as we can take time to eat consciously and nourish our bodies, we can nourish our minds too. We feed our minds "junk food" when we watch excess television, listen to the radio 24/7 and always need to be surrounded by noise, or spend mindless hours looking at social media or gossiping. Feed your mind by learning something new, like a foreign language or how to play an instrument, listening to uplifting music, or reading books, to name just a few examples.

Being mindful is no longer only for the new-age set. Neither is it only about sitting in meditation. In a digitally run, busy world, the practice of mindfulness has gained popularity and can help us to reduce our stress levels, conquer comparisons and judgments, and improve the quality of our lives overall. And it's free.

Find what quiets your mind—find what works for you.

Admit

No one is immune to the green-eyed monster. Instead of trying to hide jealousy, envy, or negative emotions, admit what it is you are feeling. Because the more we try to hide or suppress emotions, the bigger they become. It's like trying to hide a pimple with concealer: While it temporarily masks the inflamed blemish, it also clogs our pores so when we wash off the makeup, the blemish has often grown in size.

Before we can make a successful change, we first have to admit what we feel. If we avoid doing so, we risk becoming alienated from ourselves and no longer knowing who we are, what we want, or how to achieve our personal or professional goals. Admitting our negative feelings is difficult, because usually they are attached to events or thoughts that we would rather avoid or forget. Yet avoiding negative emotions only buys us a short-term gain at the price of long-term pain. We do tend to know when we are denying our emotions; the truth is present on some level, and, in the long term, this can cause constant low-grade anxiety and apprehension.

Emotional avoidance often means denying the truth—and that's not a good foundation for a healthy life, especially as the avoidance of what we're really feeling can become habitual. We can mask our negative emotions by trying to distract ourselves with any variety of external factors—alcohol and/or drug dependency, food or shopping addictions, or focusing on other people's problems instead of our own—but then what happens? Well, if we choose unhealthy distractions to relieve or avoid our stress, then we are apt to choose the same "solution" the following night, and then again and again, until it becomes a habit.

When we tune out our feelings, we avoid the important messages we are supposed to hear. We miss the important clues, our feelings, that can help us figure out who we are.

The first step in changing this pattern and letting go of our unhealthy emotions is to recognize and admit our feelings. When we do so, we open up to the reality of *what is*.

Sometimes it is painful to confront our feelings and look at them realistically and honestly, but it's an important step in coping with jealousy, envy, comparisons, judgments, and any other negative emotions. And remember, thoughts and emotions by their very nature are only ever temporary: *They, too, shall pass!* Our bodies are constantly working to regain balance and harmony, and when something is imbalanced, our bodies will let us know.

Our bodies are constantly talking to us, sending information to us through our sensations and feelings. For example, a headache may be your body's way of communicating that you are dehydrated and need to drink more water. But our bodies are not going to shout out our names over a megaphone to get our attention; we have to listen—*and listening means feeling.* The first step is admitting our feelings, and then we can begin the process of letting them go. We have to admit to and be honest about our feelings before we can let them go. *If we continue to deny them, then all we're doing is denying ourselves the chance to make a change.*

So, admit to those negative emotions and accept you are not perfect (no one is, as we learned in Chapter 7). Instead of trying to deny any unhealthy emotions, *admit* that you feel this way. Unpleasant feelings are as crucial as the enjoyable ones in helping us make sense of life's ups and downs. One of the primary reasons we have emotions in the first place is to help us evaluate our experiences.

Accepting any negative emotions, together with nonjudgmental compassion for yourself, is key to the acceptance of who you are.

Once we no longer avoid our feelings, we can choose to feel positive emotions and release the unhealthy ones. We can learn to live with an open heart, able to understand and know ourselves better, and equally important, to give and receive love. In other words, our ability to understand the value of our emotions allows us to move forward in life in a positive direction.

Acknowledge

We all have strengths and weaknesses. Our strengths are things we can leverage, and they make us stronger. So, before you read any further, grab a pen and write down at least 10 things you are good at.

Maybe you have a green thumb, are good with numbers, or are exceptional with listening. Do you make people laugh, have organizational skills, or whip up amazing dishes? Perhaps you run marathons, give motivational speeches, nurture pets, or are kind to others. Whatever is on your strengths list—big or small—it's important because *it's a unique part of who you are.*

Now, make another list and write down all the ways you've helped other people. (Or if you're a hands-on creative type, make a collage of things that you are good at, or that make you feel good.) There's not another person out there like you, and acknowledging your strengths will remind you that you add a unique touch to the world. Have confidence in the positives and know how great you really are.

It's equally important to know your weaknesses so you have the power to improve. Knowing your weaknesses gives you a clearer look at what is holding you back. So now, write down five things about yourself that you consider weaknesses. These might range from professional to social skills. Maybe you make decisions too often from a place of emotion, you give your power away to your partner or employer, or you shy away from taking healthy risks. Maybe you let your own health slide as you put everyone else's needs in front of your own.

Weaknesses can hold us back from achieving great things, but they can also help us find out more about ourselves so we can be well-rounded individuals.

Besides, there is a flip side to everything—night and day; love and hate. So, after you write down five things you consider to be your weaknesses, write down the strength/flip part to each of your personal weaknesses. *Because in every weakness lies a strength.* For example:

- shy/reflective
- emotionless/calm
- inconsistent/flexible
- disorganized/creative
- stubborn/dedicated

If you can't figure out your personal weakness/strength pairs, consult with a trusted friend or family member who might be able to offer you a different perspective, and open your eyes to the strengths in your weaknesses. It's incredible how once we know our weaknesses, this new well-rounded understanding of ourselves then *allows us to discover positives about ourselves.*

How we live our lives will depend on what we choose to focus on—light or dark, positive or negative, strength or weakness. Often we focus on what we consider "wrong" or what we don't have. Imagine how different life would be if we focused as much energy on our positive talents as we do on our *perceived* negative traits!

Nonetheless, simply *acknowledging both your strengths and weaknesses can help you shape and meet your personal goals.* Refrain from focusing *all* your energy on "fixing" your weaknesses, because discovering yourself and who you are should be more about *focusing on the positives. Be aware of your weaknesses, but focus on your strengths,* and naturally, over time, you will lead your life and make choices from a place of belief and strength.

Chapter 15

LEAD BY EXAMPLE
A Recipe for Self-belief

Without the layer of children between the world and us, life can either open up with possibilities . . . or shrink to the size of the kitchen table. Now that the children have moved out, if you haven't already, it's time to focus on what you can do for *you*. Tuck away that "Wonder Mom" cape (put it in the kiddos' box full of the special items you're saving so they can share childhood memories with their own children one day), because you don't need it anymore. It's time to flip the page and begin the next chapter of your life!

If you truly believe in yourself and in your abilities, you are going to approach your life and any upcoming issues, goals, and concerns *with a healthy sense of control*. You are going to make choices that propel you in a positive direction and impact the world with your *positive* energy and self-belief.

Believing in and valuing yourself is the key to self-purpose and happiness.

If we are in healthy control of our lives, feelings like jealousy, competitiveness, judgments, guilt, and worry become inconsequential. Sure, we still are going to feel them from time to time (that's what makes us human). But when we believe in ourselves, those emotions are short-lived. So while you may never fully rid yourself of them, *they no longer have the domineering influence they once had over your choices and your life.*

Conversely, if we relinquish our sense of healthy control and resort to an unhealthy kind of control, we are placing little to no value on our selves and our abilities. In short, this means we are not taking responsibility for our choices, our actions, and ultimately, our lives.

Over the years, when we immersed ourselves in raising our children, it was common to tie our value to our children by meeting their needs and feeling needed by them. When they were successful, by extension we felt successful. When they made the wrong choices, by extension we felt responsible, and our self-esteem took the hit. But when we do this, our self-confidence vacillates, making it hard to form a solid core of self-belief. The greatest gift we can give to our children (grown or otherwise), and the greatest gift we can give to ourselves, is positive self-belief.

Where does self-belief start?

With you, leading by example.

Creating Self-belief

You can move mountains if you believe in yourself. You can live in happiness, and you can live with optimism, motivation, responsibility, and positivity. With self-belief comes freedom: the freedom to make mistakes and see them as lessons; the freedom to deserve happiness . . . *your OWN happiness.* So listen up, retired moms!

Self-belief helps us facilitate creative solutions to our concerns and issues, find paths to our dreams and goals, and perceive opportunities that otherwise would go unnoticed. What better gift is there than for you to feel this personally, and moreover, to know it also directly affects *your child* in a positive way? It's a win-win situation. So say goodbye to dreadful guilt, unruly emotions, and the green-eyed monster. It takes some hard work and elbow grease to scrub yourself clean of deep-seated negative emotions, but just like with any chore, the hardest part is getting started.

Self-belief is not something we can purchase to arrive second-day air from Amazon. We won't find it in the grocery store produce aisle, or conveniently hanging in the mall next to some fashionable pieces of clothing.

> **Acquiring self-belief is a step-by-step process that takes desire and perseverance.**

You need to be mentally prepared and physically able to take on this challenge. Not perfect, but simply *willing to take on a risk that is healthy for yourself.*

Now that your children are out of the nest, it's time to challenge yourself and deliberately think about yourself, your identity, and your goals and dreams in more constructive ways. If you have a bit of self-love and an ounce of hope, I am going to help you create your ideal recipe for building belief in yourself, and in what you can do to enjoy this new chapter of your life.

Recipe for Self-belief

Total time: Months to decades (each person's dish will vary slightly in terms of outcome; do not attempt last-minute overnight fiascos)

Level: Moderate to hard

Serves: *You*

Ingredients

Responsibility for yourself—add extra yeast to make rise

Experimentation in life—add sugar and spice, and everything nice

Juices of patience and perseverance

Compassion zest

Several cups of intention

Directions

1. Develop an action plan and mix by hand.

2. Stick to it—do not grease pan.

3. Combine patience and perseverance, then whisk in compassion. For best results, repeat this step multiple times, adding more as needed.

4. Don't wait—no preheating needed.

5. Serve warm or cold. Share with a friend.

6. Enjoy!

Not your typical 15-minute chicken-and-rice casserole, but a dish sure to feed your soul and be a crowd-pleaser.

Rise Up and Take Responsibility for Yourself

Yeast is the magical ingredient that allows a dense mass of dough to become a well-risen loaf of bread. In bakeries and home kitchens, there are several categories of baking yeast available. There is active dry yeast, compressed cake yeast or fresh yeast, quick-rise yeast, and even instant yeast. The wisdom the baker needs is to know which yeast will work best for their desired result.

You are the baker of your own process, so you need to find what you need to rise up and take responsibility for your life.

All of us live in a culture of impatience and immediate gratification afforded by technology, fast-food joints, and overnight deliveries. Instant gratification is the need to experience fulfillment without the wait. If we think about it, anything can be delivered, and fast: food, flowers, furniture, answers from Google; even people are just a fingertip touch away, via online dating sites, social media sites, and so on. But instant gratification comes at a price—*it makes us less patient.*

In life, it's tempting to go for the fast, the immediate gratification, the instant yeast. The demand for instantaneous feedback leads to a society that experiences fewer waits but creates habits that can slowly lead to us possessing less and less patience.

Yet whether raising children, climbing the professional ladder, pursuing our passions, or teaching others, there is no way around slow, sometimes agonizing, growth.

We also live in a world where we have become too dependent on others. It's easy to give up our responsibility and our power when we are conditioned to seek help from external sources. We don't have to learn to fix a tire; we can call AAA. Instead of learning to read a map, we can rely on Siri or Waze to get us to our destination. We may even put our happiness in the hands of our significant others, thinking that will bring us fulfillment. We may be fearful of being alone (forgetting the value and pleasure that can be found in solitude), experiencing rejection (because we are too used to constant social contact and partnership), and making decisions (which involves taking responsibility). All this leaves us reliant on others.

- **Taking personal responsibility means investing in ourselves, and this takes time and patience.** Taking personal responsibility is like adding warm water to a packet of yeast. The organisms in that packet lie dormant until they come in contact with warm water, and once activated, they begin to make the dough rise slowly, with good results. In a similar way, many of us too have been lying dormant; as moms of children, we put ourselves aside, sometimes for years.

- **We are responsible for our own selves, whether we like it or not.** We are born alone, and we die alone, so we each have to take responsibility for our lives, every step of the way. Until, and unless, we accept responsibility for our actions, it will be difficult to for us to develop self-respect, or respect for others.

- **Taking conscious control of our responses to the circumstances and events in our lives is empowering.** This kind of control is healthy: it helps us naturally feel like we deserve more as our self-value builds and we feel better about our very selves.

This is important because most often it's our very selves who are standing in the way of our happiness and success!

We do this by:

- having unrealistic expectations
- doubting our own abilities
- looking for approval
- holding on to the past

- making excuses (the big one!)

Have you ever tried explaining why you "couldn't," "shouldn't," or "wouldn't" do something? Each one of us, at one time or another, has made an excuse for not acting or initiating. Maybe we missed a deadline at work; maybe we didn't pursue our dream of competing in a marathon or living in another country for a time. When relying on excuses becomes a habit for us, we project that we are not dependable to others, and we're seen as unmotivated, lazy, dreamers, or defensive.

Making excuses instead of taking 100 percent responsibility for their actions and circumstances is the main reason people fail to succeed in their personal and professional lives. We need to learn to make decisions on our own, and to be comfortable with our choices. If we want to put an end to excuses and take responsibility for our lives, we need to step up and focus on our goals—big and small.

Life shouldn't just be about *big* events and future choices; we need to take responsibility *in everyday life*. This can involve small choices, like what food we put in our body during a particular meal, or how we organize our day. Doing so requires self-discipline, for we are making a commitment to continuous self-improvement.

Of course, we can expect to encounter challenges when we begin taking responsibility for our choices. Remember, it's not something we are going to master over a three-day weekend . . . so what are we waiting for? Why not start *now?*

As you embark on the process, recognize there is no quick fix or shortcut when it comes to taking personal responsibility. Adding more yeast to dough will give a faster rise—but this can have negative results. The dough may rise too fast and create too much gluten, making the dough collapse. In the same way, there are no good shortcuts in terms of taking responsibility. Temporarily it may work . . . but the end result is never good. *At the end of the day, we only have our own selves to fall back on.*

Taking personal responsibility is what produces authentic, long-lasting, and positive results in life.

Experimentation in Life—Sugar and Spice and Everything Nice

It's time to spice up your life and have some fun! Get your sexy *on.* Get the passion back in your life. Feel youthful and alive by experiencing life.

Lead by Example

Risk-taking behavior is part of normal youth development: It helps a young person develop decision-making skills and build confidence. This is what drives a toddler to take their first steps, or a teen to learn to drive. Without taking risks, children will never reach their desired results. However, as we age, our desire to take healthy risks may diminish. This is because we are creatures of habit, and we feel safe and secure in the comfort of our daily routines. We tend to resist too much excitement, even if it's what we long for. But with the kids out of the house now, and without you having to worry about them and their needs constantly, it's time to embark on a little risk of your own.

Have you ever thought, *I'm stuck in a rut?* If you are awash in the daily routine of going to work, shopping for groceries, and cooking meals, life can get a little dull. You may not even notice the "dulling" at first because over time, it can creep in slowly—in between raising children, putting in some long hours at work, and juggling the rest of life. Ask yourself:

- Is the fun missing in your life right now?
- Does your career bother you in terms of experiencing chronic tension and stress?
- Has the love-and-marriage routine become boring for you?

• Are you sick of being in your house day in, day out? If you're answering "yes" to any of these or similar questions, then maybe your life calls for a change.

Please know you don't have to do or be something dramatically different to make your life more exciting. But if your life is too predictable, it can feel boring. To increase your quota of happiness, you will need to find a balance between comfort and adventure.

Maybe you always wanted to travel the world, or try something new, like playing the oboe, sculpting, or skydiving. Experimenting is so important because it shows you what is not working so you can progress to the next thing that is working.

I am ready to acknowledge, though, that living an exciting life sounds fun in theory, but it can be a bit daunting to face the possibility of actually doing something to make it full of sugar and spice. To shift away from this mindset, you might like to start out by trying one new thing each day. It can be as simple as taking the subway to work instead of a cab, ordering a new dish at a restaurant, or selecting a new hobby or exercise class to try. Once you do, you will feel new emotions and different feelings that will make for an interesting experience.

When you've done that, you'll be ready to go for something bigger—plan a road trip with your best friend or book a vacation. Traveling is the quickest way to get excited and stimulated by life again because it means seeing, smelling, feeling, and experiencing new things. Seeing new places opens your eyes and inspires your senses. On your travels, you can also make new friends and meet new acquaintances. Adventure helps us see things with a fresh perspective and opens the door for us to reenergize our lives with more fun and creativity. One day the final curtain will be drawn, and you don't want to experience any lingering *I could have*, or *I should have* thoughts. Nobody wants to look back at their life and reminisce about how predictable and boring it was.

You get one life—appreciate it and make the most of it.

Experience is more than just the spice of life. It's the secret ingredient, that "little something" that expands your senses and makes your life more fulfilling. Life is too short—it's up to you to make it sweet.

Juices of Patience and Perseverance

You might have noticed that things don't always happen when you want them to. Sometimes, in between wanting something to happen and the actual happening, you freak out.

WARNING: Frustration happens!

Three Squeezes of Patience

What is the purpose of adding the juice of *patience* to our lives? Happiness, better relationships, and more success. Exercising patience is a lifelong spiritual practice—as well as a way to find emotional freedom.

Every day there are reasons to be impatient: traffic, telemarketers, grocery lines, people not doing what they say they're going to. Resentment. Disappointment. We can live in frustration—drive ourselves crazy, attempting to control every outcome or being cranky—or learn to transform frustration with patience.

Using the following three squeezes of patience, you can help create more happiness in your life:

1. Be Mindful of What Makes You Feel Rushed

Our mental to-do lists can become like a jammed blender in our brains. We are so occupied with what we need to do, we feel stuck and impatient. Revisit Chapters 12 and 14 for more on awareness and mindfulness.

2. Practice Gratitude

Thankfulness has a multitude of benefits, including making us feel happier, less stressed, and more optimistic. I keep a calendar, and for each day I write down something I'm thankful for: my health, my family, a massage, my home, the vacation to Alaska coming up, the sunflowers in my garden, the food on my table . . . the list goes on. Not a day goes by that I don't think of something I'm grateful for.

3. Embrace the Uncomfortable

We're so used to being comfortable that we can feel like we should be in a state of adjustment when we're out of our comfort zone. But, discomfort or change has its purposes and helps push us to find solutions. When I tore my ACL and MCL and partially fractured my tibia, I was jacked up on crutches for five months. The doctors didn't know why my leg would not straighten or bend; it was locked. Being the physical person I am, at first, I felt confined and limited. However, this pushed me to move past my "comfort zone" and change the daily routines (and habits) with which I was so familiar and comfortable.

I adapted to teaching martial arts on crutches (yup, it worked about as well as it sounds, but I had to make do and I did). And it changed my priorities, helping me see what was really important. The brown easy chair became my new best friend, and I started writing this book. I also created a series of Action Awareness Training webinars that I began to teach on Zoom from home. The injury helped me to find patience in my embracing the situation rather than fighting the uncomfortable feelings it brought, and it has since been a huge blessing in disguise.

By embracing discomfort, we naturally cultivate more patience. Our long-term personal growth depends on it. Patience allows us to restrain judgment long enough to make informed decisions, which helps pave the path to a healthy and happy life. So . . . add as much patience as needed. Mix. Add more.

Hint: It takes more than you think. If the mixture looks dry and crumbly, however frustrating it may be, *don't give up!* It will work if you continue to add *patience*—and follow up with a long juicy squeeze of *perseverance.*

A Squeeze of Perseverance

Successful people never give up. They have a "don't quit" attitude that sustains them when they encounter the inevitable roadblocks and setbacks. They keep trying, working, and persisting long after the average person has thrown in the towel. They *persevere* to the end.

So, persevere—and be patient as you do so!

Compassion Zest

A grate of compassion zest gives us the ability to care for ourselves. Instead of just ignoring our pain, we stop and tell ourselves, "This is really difficult right now. How can I *comfort and care for myself* in this moment?" Maybe it's spending the afternoon at the lake or taking a warm bath. Maybe it's wrapping up in a cozy blanket and reading a good book. Or going to the spa and pampering yourself with a relaxing facial or massage. Whatever it is, put that ingredient into your life and do something positive just for *you!*

A sprinkle of *compassion zest* is a must to help our newfound patience and perseverance turn into self-belief.

Together, these ingredients make a liquid sure to appease the taste buds. And remember, before throwing the towel in, we can always add more as needed.

Directions

1. Mix by hand—develop an action plan

Eggs, flour, sugar, and cream of tartar, the ingredients needed to bake an angel food cake, may be sitting on your countertop, but simply staring at them will not magically turn them into a cake. They remain separate ingredients until *you make a plan of action to combine these ingredients and mix them together.* It's the same with your thoughts: You may have many dreams and ideas right in front of you on the kitchen table, but until you put them into action, they will remain untouched and inactive right there in front of you.

Your life is truly in *your* hands. Developing an action plan can turn dreams and aspirations into reality and increase your accountability and efficiency. There is an inspirational adage that says, "People don't plan to fail. Instead they fail to plan." It is not hard to set a goal. The true challenge is *creating and following an action plan to turn that goal into a reality.*

Lead by Example

I'll share with you an action plan that I've been working on to build my self-belief. (And I wrote "working on" because it truly is a process!)

To build self-belief, it's important to first know who you are and what you want. Because when we struggle in terms of believing in ourselves, it's common to filter out the positive aspects of ourselves and focus on the negatives. Instead:

1. **Start by identifying, and focusing on, the positive aspects of yourself.** Consciously work to identify and acknowledge your strengths and talents. Maybe you are a good friend to others, you have a particular skill set, you can make others laugh, you have a good work ethic, or you can dance, paint, or speak in front of large groups. Then, after you figure out who you are at this moment in time, move on to the next step.

2. **Ask yourself, "What do I want?"** I'm not talking about that red dress at Nordstrom, or a desire to eat chocolate for breakfast. What do you really want out of life? Self-belief? Success? Happiness? What are your goals and dreams? Maybe they are the same as when you were a teenager, or maybe they've shifted over the years. Probably you've accomplished many

things already (that's amazing!) and now you're at a time of your life where you can do even more. Whatever it is that you want personally out of life, isn't it time to get started?

3. **Start small but get started in achieving what you want out of life.** Starting is often more difficult than it seems, especially if you have a hard time making decisions in the first place. You may experience the constant fear that your decision could be the wrong choice, so you make no decision at all. Or, you end up doing nothing at all because you're afraid that you won't do enough when you do.

Great things start *small*. Even if you have a huge vision for your life, you have a bigger chance of successfully achieving it if you start with small actions. These baby steps act like they are stepping-stones toward reaching your vision. After all, you need the right habits to support your ambitions—and habits are born out of *consistency*.

If you need to take more responsibility for your actions to develop belief in yourself, start small. Investing in yourself starts with little things, like achieving some private relaxation time through taking a warm bath, reading a book, or doing something just for you. When you set a small goal, your subconscious mind offers less resistance on the path to it—since you don't perceive it as a threat or challenge, you'll find it easier to complete.

As you embark on your journey of self-belief and goal-achievement, you will grow and evolve, so the goals you choose for yourself may shift. As you go through different seasons, your priorities may change. Yet no matter where you are in your goal-making process, success is a series of small tasks put in action by *you.*

2. Do not grease pan—stick to it

"Greasy" guilt, worry, and other negative emotions are things we don't need, but if you slip off the cookie sheet before your cookie is baked, it's okay—it happens to all of us at one time or another. So instead of beating yourself up for days or giving in, acknowledge you made a mistake, then jump right back onboard. Get right back up and on that sheet and stick to it with your intention. *Because the only person who can make self-belief happen for you is you.*

Women who believe in themselves:

- don't let a bad hair day ruin their afternoon

- don't let their moon cycles rule their reactions

- don't let some extra pounds crush date night

- and they certainly never give up

Instead, they set their intentions.

The power of intention . . . you've probably heard of it. Everything starts with intention.

If you want to bake cookies, wiggle your toes, or text someone, it all starts with an intention. If you start the day without an intention of how you'd like it to go, or what you'd like to accomplish that day, it's like boarding a plane with no clue where it's headed. A little bit of this is okay because fate has your back, but *if you want to go somewhere or reach something, the power of intention is what is going to help you get there.*

Don't forget to add this key "ingredient" into your new life to help you aim, create, and "stick to it" until you reach your desired outcome.

Living life without intention is like attempting to make a meringue without cream of tartar—it becomes a flop. When added to egg whites, cream of tartar denatures some of the egg protein, making the whites foam and expand up to eight times their original size. Not only does this add volume, but it also stabilizes the outcome. *Setting intentions will do the same for you.*

Your intention could be specific—having a quality conversation today with your child or having a beneficial meeting with your boss—or broader, like bettering your health, or becoming more mindful.

Here are some examples of intentions to help build your self-belief:

- I set my intention to take responsibility for my health and well-being.
- I set my intention to do one nice thing for myself each day.
- I set my intention to make someone smile today.
- I set my intention to focus on the positive.
- I set my intention to allow opportunity into my life.
- I set my intention to be open to change.
- I set my intention to value and appreciate myself and others.
- I set my intention to love myself.

You can say an intention (or intentions) one time in the morning before you start your day. Or, maybe add your intention to your meditation or yoga practice. Perhaps say it when you first awaken, bringing in the energy of the words and holding it in your heart for a few seconds. Maybe you write the intention down in a journal each morning, or on your calendar. Whichever way you decide works best for you, the act of setting intentions will allow you to focus on who you are in the moment, and to recognize and live your value. This raises the frequency of your energy emotionally and physically.

Imagine the changes that can take place within the mind and body as you begin to consciously give intention to positive choices. This goes far beyond you, since your positive energy has an extremely beneficial impact on all those around you.

3. *Add love—mix in patience, perseverance, and compassion*

For some recipes, mixing ingredients out of order can cause unwanted chemical reactions or make the right reactions happen at the wrong time, or incompletely, or not at all. In any event, it introduces unnecessary variability in the carefully thought-out procedure of the recipe. For example, when making yeast bread, scones, muffins, or quick breads, it's important to combine dry ingredients separately from the liquid ingredients to avoid one single mushy lump. However, for the self-belief recipe, you don't have to be so picky about the order in which you mix in your liquids.

Naturally our patience, perseverance, and compassion don't happen all at once—they rise over time and through experiences. When mixing together your self-belief ingredients, you don't have to worry, as you might with other recipes, about an overflow of liquid saturating the creamed butter and causing the mixture to separate and result in a tougher cake. In fact, it's quite the opposite, so go right ahead and mix in as much juice of patience and perseverance and zest of compassion as possible. Because it comes down to this:

You can't mix enough patience, perseverance, and compassion into the recipe of self-belief. Go ahead, mix it in, you're going to be one tough cookie.

4. Don't wait—no preheating necessary

For some recipes it's a good idea to preheat the oven and get the right temperature from the get-go. However, *when cultivating self-belief, preheating is unnecessary and a waste of time and energy.*

A mistake I witness moms make time and time again (and one of my personal procrastinations, too) is *waiting* to do things. And if you ask any of these moms what they are waiting for, they come up with a list of well-thought-out excuses (as I have in the past).

I've known Lynn for more than 10 years. She is an incredible writer who loves to tell stories. Seven years ago, when her children still lived at home, I asked her when she was going to write a book. Her reply was one I hear often from mothers: "When the kids are older, I'll have time for myself."

Last week (seven years later) I met up with Lynn, and I told her I was excited to hear how her passion of writing was going now that her four children had moved out.

Lynn looked at me and shrugged her shoulders. "Probably after the grandkids are grown will be a good time to start," she said in a nonchalant tone.

I did a quick calculation and realized she would be 67 by then—by no means too old to start. But the important question is, why not start *now?* Today. Whether your child is young or grown, why not follow your passions and dreams now? Inspire yourself, and inspire your grown children at the same time, by leading by example.

This is your life, and *your chance is right now.* You may have made a choice years ago to have children, but that doesn't mean you have to forfeit your dreams and passions. If you put your life on hold, telling yourself it's "just until the kids are moved out or married" or "until the grandkids are grown," the final curtain will be drawn before you know it!

Lead by Example

Don't wait for the moon to drop out of the constellation Gemini so you can star-hop over to Castor and Pollux from Orion. Don't wait for the perfect moment or the burning bush before doing something for you—because it doesn't just happen. You have to *make it happen*. And there is no better time to start than now.

You don't have to be ready. You just have to be willing.

Stop worrying about the future and regretting the past and do what you can do at this very moment. Start where you are; it's the most basic step you can take.

Now, what is one thing you can do right now to act on this idea?

If you want to be a writer, write one paragraph. If you want to be a web designer, create one photoshop image. If you want to lose ten pounds, put on your running shoes and open the door.

Moms are good at figuring out what everyone else in the household needs to be happy. We have a knack for organizing everyone else's hectic lives. But sometimes we forget to take care of *us*. We forget about deciding what it is *we* really want.

The time for you is now—not tomorrow.

Time waits for no one. Life keeps moving with or without you, and it can make your decisions for you when you're too slow. **Instead of letting life rule you, take charge of life.** Forget about preheating and waiting for the perfect moment. Just go for it—start today so there is time to have your cake and eat it too.

5. Serve warm or cold–share with a friend

We don't have to eat our cake alone. As we cultivate self-belief and deal with change in our lives, our friends can help us weather the ups and downs in life. Sometimes we may doubt our own decisions and abilities, but our true friends never do. Even in the ugliest of situations, they help us.

They also believe in us—that we will make it through with confidence—and can provide a sounding board and place for us to grow. There are plenty of instances and decisions that will require key solo time and self-reflection, but equally important is time in which we can happily socialize. So reach out to a friend or a mentor, especially at times when your self-belief recipe proves confusing or difficult to follow.

Everyone, even retired Wonder Moms, needs companionship and a shoulder on which to lean.

Good friends bring special meaning to our lives. Just as we hope for and encourage our children to hang out with peers who are positive influences, we as adults should surround ourselves with those who have a huge positive impact on us. That might sound like common sense, but it can be surprising whom we invite to the kitchen table of friendship.

With a good friend, we can create great conversations, share a tear, or have laugh-out-loud fun. We can talk about big events, spouses, and, of course, the kids. We can share our embarrassing moments and funny stories. Friends fill our hearts with care, support, and motivation, and help us to cope with challenges and celebrate life. Real friendship has true healing power.

And, when it comes down to it, *cultivating belief in yourself is really about developing the skills needed to be your own best friend.* Ultimately the longest, most important relationship you will ever have throughout your life is with yourself—and this relationship is a gift that no one can ever take away from you. That's why it's so important to be able to rely on your own judgment, as then you can be your own source of comfort. You can be your own cheerleader, your own coach.

Self-belief gives us flexible thinking, which allows for a shift in perspective and finds the quiet in the chaos. We learn to trust our own words when we speak to ourselves. We may be honest with ourselves without sugarcoating the truth.

Self-belief helps us reconcile external changes, integrate internal goals, and balance inconsistencies. We are responsible; we determine how outside factors influence our inner sense of value. *This means when our child-rearing days are over, and the nest is empty, we don't have to feel bare inside.*

So it's time to ramp up the focus on self, and the search for *our* personal interests. We did our jobs as "Mom," and now it's time to retire and make decisions focused around us, and our dreams for ourselves. We can set goals and achieve what *we* want.

6. Enjoy!

Live life for *you*. Explore your hopes and dreams for the future. Then put them into action.

The future just became now.

Chapter 16

"ARE THE KIDS ALL WE HAVE IN COMMON?"
Reconnecting

Once the kids move out, there's this sense for many moms that we've . . . *outgrown* where we are in life. We're ready for something new, something deeper. Something that's more aligned with the person we are becoming, and the truth of our purpose.

When we launch our children into the real world, there's no doubt we launch our own massive transition too. One of the biggest fears faced by the married women I interviewed was *how their relationship or marriage would adapt once the children left home.* Many expressed concern that after decades of being together, all they had in common these days with their partner was the children.

Just as their identity changed from wife/partner to mother once their baby arrived, so their relationship identity with their romantic partner may have changed (often without their conscious realization!) from that of lovers to parents. Texts that were once flirty were replaced with grocery lists. Going out on dates transitioned to driving the kids to and attending their soccer games. The arrival of children is hard on marriages, and while the departure of children makes it easier for some couples, others may come to find they have nothing in common to hold their relationship together anymore.

With the kids out of the house, it's time to reinvent your love together, set new goals, and turn the page. Another new chapter awaits, and since you are the author of your book, you can make it as cheerful or dismal as you choose. You alone are in control of your happiness meter. You are responsible for the outcome.

My Story

Before my husband and I were married, the preacher sat us down in his office and proceeded to explain to us the four pillars it takes to build a happy and lasting relationship. I was 24 at the time, not really a churchgoer, and with the wedding two days away and a to-do list longer than my angel-cut wedding veil with satin ribbon, the last thing I wanted to do was sit down and listen to some speech. At that time I was in love, and in my opinion, I pretty much had life figured out. Besides, Tony and I both had been married once before, and so we had some marital experience under our belts. We were consciously deciding to raise our children together, blend our families, and live a happy life. *How hard could it be?*

I will never forget the preacher looking us in the eye and saying softly but with emphasis, "I can tell you love each other and care for each other. That's good, because one thing you can count on in a relationship is that storms will come. You will open your umbrella, brave the weather, and with love, you will survive."

And in case we didn't hear it, he said again (more loudly this time), "storms will come."

At the time it didn't feel like any such thing would happen, but I guess the preacher did know a thing or two, because he was right. Sometimes the storm came like a high wind gently swaying the treetops, and sometimes there was a rainy downpour and flash floods. A storm did come—and then another, and another.

My husband and I lived through the challenges of raising a blended family and keeping a stable relationship, but it wasn't until approximately 18 months before our youngest moved to Los Angeles that we realized the need to strengthen our bonds if we wanted to be truly happy together in the upcoming transition. Over the years, we found we had become more involved in individual endeavors.

It all started with my heavy daily involvement in raising the kids, and Tony's dedication to the financial side of things. We spent less time together as a couple as we tried to make ends meet, and even as the children were older and hanging out with us less, we forgot sometimes to make time for us as a couple. It was easy to go on autopilot and remain focused on the daily routine; before we knew it, a couple of months would pass on by and my husband and I hadn't been on a single date together. Sure, we were cordial to each other and laughed with each other, but sometimes it felt like we were roommates instead of partners, living separate lives under the same roof.

What it came down to was a mutual decision that we didn't want to live like that. We asked ourselves if we would be better off separating or making a change to bring happiness and success into our relationship. For us, the decision was an easy one—we wanted to stay together—but the actual and necessary changes proved more difficult. With patience and perseverance (remember those two important ingredients?) we did it—and we continue to work on our relationship each and every day.

So, the preacher proved right:

Storms will come whether you are ready for them or not.

The Four Pillars of a Healthy Relationship

The preacher was right about something else too. On that same day, two days before the wedding, he shared with my husband and me that he had married hundreds of couples, *and the ones with healthy relationships that survived the storm were built upon four pillars.*

It just so happens that the four pillars have played a most meaningful part in building my relationship with my husband into one of inspiration and happiness. (Listening does pay off.) The four pillars are:

1. communication
2. intimacy
3. financial health
4. spiritual health

Pillar 1: Communication

During the first few years he spent with me, my husband communicated with me through talking, talking, and more talking. I, on the other hand, was shyer, and kept too much to myself. The preacher saw this from the moment he first met us, and so in his wisdom he said to us, "Communication does not mean talking. It means *listening*. That's why God gave us two ears and one mouth." When I heard this, I nudged my soon-to-be-husband under the table, to make sure he was hearing this part.

The preacher continued. "To communicate, you have to listen to each other. Not only to words, but also to the feeling behind the words in order to hear what the other person really needs."

Communication is the art of listening.

There is a comfortable simplicity in winning or giving up, but with dialogue and listening, no one is trying to be competitive. There is no need for someone to be right or wrong; instead, you are seeking to try to appreciate and understand the other person, which in turn helps your partner understand and validate you. *Healthy communication helps you meet your needs and stay connected in your relationship.*

That being said, every couple has a particular style of communication, and different styles can lead a couple's relationship down drastically different paths. However, a couple naturally alternates from one style of communication to another during the relationship. This is a normal part of a relationship, and healthy as long as a couple aspires to return eventually to the most intimacy-full version of which they are capable. Do you know and understand what your style of couple communication is at the moment, along with its strengths and weaknesses?

Five Styles of Couple Communication

1. **The couple who avoid arguments** tend to avoid conflict by either being silent or saying what they think the other person wants to hear. This couple may connect occasionally, but at any sign of conflict they disconnect.

2. **The silent couple** makes small talk—perhaps about the weather, meal plans, current events, or other surface issues. Rarely does this couple share emotions, feelings, or anything personal.

3. **The friends couple** get along well and typically enjoy each other's company. Their communication may be open and honest on many levels. They may

work well around the house and in business together, but one or both partners may avoid deep intimate emotional or physical intimacy.

4. **The fighting couple** has a relationship based on arguments and trying to prove the other person wrong. Generally this is a relationship in crisis where any communication focuses on what is wrong, and blame is often placed on the other person. In this kind of relationship, the power is often unbalanced: One partner feels shy to speak their feelings, whereas the other speaks to be authoritative and caress their ego. The one who has greater power within the relationship is more likely to make assumptions and be less aware of the other person's feelings or opinions. Those who remain quieter may suppress their feelings, which often results in the emotions of frustration and anger (which they often direct toward their partner). These power imbalances can interfere with the ability to listen to each other by closing down some avenues of discussion.

5. **The fully intimate couple** communicates openly about almost anything, including their deep-seated beliefs, desires, dreams, mistakes, childhood memories, finances, past relationships, and personal

goals. They do not fear emotional or physical intimacy and are transparent when they believe something is wrong. This kind of communication style takes daily awareness and work to maintain, and perhaps for this reason, the other four communication styles are more prevalent. However, complete intimacy can occur as long as both partners are clear on what they need individually and as a couple. (This is why it's so important to know yourself—who you are and what you want—first and foremost. Self-awareness is the foundation to happiness, whether it's finding the joy in your career, family, or relationships.)

Building communication skills is essential to enjoying a successful relationship. Learning to communicate openly and clearly can take work, but most people can learn how. Those who find it hard to talk to their partner may need time and encouragement to express their views. However, through sharing interests, ideas, and concerns with their partner, as well as affection, they can develop a trust that helps build mutual appreciation and companionship.

Seven Tips for Improving Communication in a Relationship

1. **Give 100 percent of your attention** to your partner when the two of you are talking. These days, everything may feel like it's battling for your attention—your phone, your emails, your health, your coworkers, your family. Silence your devices, turn away from the computer screen or television, stop multitasking, and don't let any distractions interrupt your focus on your partner. Doing this shows respect for the other person and improves listening skills.

2. **Talk face-to-face.** Most communication is less about what we say and more about how we say it. Nonverbal signals sent via our body language play an important role in how our partners react to our words. Looking at a person face-to-face, with eye contact, is a powerful way to demonstrate that you're actively listening and builds stronger communication.

3. **Find the "right time"** to share. Sometimes you think you need to be heard at this very moment, but knowing the right time, and the perfect moment, for sharing is a critical part of successful communication.

You don't want to start an important conversation as you are walking out the door to work. Or, if your partner is a morning person, you should refrain from talking about important issues late at night. So know your partner and know you. Be sensitive to moods and schedules. Be smart with timing, but also don't wait too long and allow issues to fester and turn into something bigger.

4. **Don't "attack" the other person (ever).** If, as you discuss things with your partner, you give vent to a series of attacks and criticisms (e.g., "You idiot!" "That's a stupid thought!" "What a baby you are!") or overgeneralize ("You never understand me!"), your partner will shut down and disengage. You can get your point across without putting your partner down and being hostile. Communication should bring you and your partner closer together, breaking down barriers between you rather than building barricades.

5. **Take a breather.** If you get really angry about something, stop, take a step back, and breathe. In other words: stop, look, listen (see Chapter 6). Tell your partner you need to take a break and calm down. Taking a break can help keep heated

conversations from worsening. Come back to the conversation when your mind is collected and your emotions have cooled. From this state, you're more likely to have success turning conflict into collaboration.

6. **Focus on now.** To listen fully, you have to engage and be fully present. If you've stopped talking for a moment but all the things you still want to say are circling around in your head, it's hard to really listen to what the other person is saying. Stay in the now, keep focused on the topic at hand, and avoid using "cheap shots" from the past that will only add fuel to the fire. By focusing on each other—right now and what's in front of you today—communication becomes more natural.

7. **Forgive.** Forgiving your partner if they've done something that hurt, disappointed, or betrayed you is one of the hardest things. For this reason, many people hold grudges and past resentments that last a lifetime. Negativity builds bitterness and insult, and no one wins when pain is left unresolved. Don't let your relationship suffer because you are re-experiencing prior frustration and resentment—whether perceived or real—about the times when

your partner "wronged" you in the past. Forgiveness is a skill that involves vulnerability and is built over time. Start by letting go of the small conflicts that can chafe a relationship, and you'll discover fewer colossal conflicts will arise. Forgiveness helps us move beyond the emotion of the moment and consider how we want our long-term relationship to be in the future. It allows us to move beyond the issue, and to heal and grow.

Pillar 2: Intimacy

When we think of *intimacy,* we often think of physical intimacy. There are times when we hunger for a sexual connection, and yet it also requires our trust and vulnerability to allow someone into our most personal space.

Sexual connection is a healthy part of a relationship when it's about making love—sharing a passionate and intimate connection—instead of the sole act of sex. Intimacy is not only about sharing parts; more importantly, it's about sharing hearts.

Sexual connection is part of a healthy relationship, and equally important is the emotional and intellectual intimacy where we share a meeting of the minds. When we seek an emotional bond, we want to share our tough times and our successes. We want to be cuddled, loved, and accepted for who we are. In a relationship, we crave a deep emotional connection with our partner, and a feeling that is all about closeness, trust, and comfort. Yet we can be with a partner for years and never reach emotional intimacy, staying at an arm's length to avoid uncomfortable feelings of vulnerability and transparency.

> **Authentic intimacy can be found and reached, although it's better if we think it as less of a destination, and more of an experience.**

Communication, as addressed above, is a key to growing a couple's intimacy. A relationship sown with awareness and understanding can bloom into an intimate connection of something profoundly special: a mutual respect, and an unconditional love.

Pillar 3: Financial health

Affluence means different things to different people, partly depending on how they were raised, what they want out of life, and their beliefs and values. Financial issues are at the top of the list of reasons most relationships break up.

Financial harmony is also critical in creating a relationship based on respect, validation, power, freedom, and happiness. In successful relationships, partners discuss and set guidelines and boundaries for their financial decisions.

Learning to talk about money and work together as a team not only improves financial intimacy, but also may salvage a relationship.

Before my husband and I started on our financial journey, I was considered the homemaker in charge of raising our three children, and he was the breadwinner. Yes, I was thankful I could spend time each day with the children without needing to use daycare, but always in the back of my mind, I felt inadequate that I wasn't contributing more financially to our family—and this challenged my self-worth.

We therefore had separate financial goals, and because we didn't invite each other to look at our finances together as players on the same team, it was hard to make much headway in our savings. It wasn't until years later, when the children began to move out and we suddenly realized time was passing us by at an alarming rate, that we began to work on our financial plan together—and see tangible results.

This was easier said than done, though. At first my husband didn't much like the thought of budgeting: He said it made him feel "too controlled" when he was the one bringing in the money. On the other hand, I liked to budget, but I'd become discouraged after previous failed attempts. So we had to communicate—yes, communication once again, and lots of it—to come to a mutual decision about what was needed and what we wanted financially. Then we looked at the reality of what we had to do to get there. Once we established our financial goals, we made a budget, and started paying off our debts and building up our savings. Starting with paying off the smallest credit card balance and working up to the largest, we now have a solid retirement plan and financial goals that are being met.

Working as a team and having equal knowledge and say in the finances gives us strength and belief as a couple to expand and excel in other areas of our life.

Now my husband and I "fist-bump" when we pay a bill, transfer $50 of our savings into our vacation account, or save a dollar on milk. The topic that used to provoke underlying currents of agitation and tension in our relationship has become a fun goal to achieve and celebrate together.

Pillar 4: Spiritual health

The spiritual component of a relationship is what everything else in the relationship revolves around. *Spiritual intimacy* is how we can effectively appreciate our lives, respond to relationship issues, and handle transitions and life challenges.

Many people get into relationships to satisfy their own personal needs, but when two people come together with the intention to love and learn, an evolution of deep satisfaction and long-term fulfillment arises. The spiritual pillar provides healing and well-being and makes us feel whole.

Most of us believe in a "higher power," whether it be God, Mother Nature, the universe, energy, or something else. As we continue through our lives, the desire for a deeper spiritual connection often follows. It's less about practicing a certain religion or being a person of a particular faith, and more about our connection to self and to something higher.

As a young boy, my husband was raised in the Catholic Church—he was dropped off curbside (going to

Mass on his own) each Sunday—whereas I was raised in nature, surrounded by the natural world. Although he and I had very different upbringings, both of us carry a common deep-seated appreciation for "something higher" and a similar sense as to what is "right" and what is "wrong." How to grow together spiritually was a little less obvious.

Upon combining our families, my husband and I decided to say a prayer of gratitude each day with the children. Giving a simple thanks and acknowledging all the good in our lives each day made us more thoughtful and gave us collectively an increased sense of awareness of a higher presence.

Over the years, my husband and I have collected practices that benefit us individually and as a couple that facilitate a greater faith. Our morning starts with an active meditation to help set our intentions for the day ahead, and we also keep a calendar-journal comprised of special moments throughout the day and our future personal and joint goals.

Spirituality helps nurture our relationships by creating a deeper understanding of our lives and our loved ones. Sharing our appreciation of each other with our partners and enjoying spiritual endeavors together can be reached through taking a walk in nature, holding hands, and focusing on the beauty around us. It can be found together through helping others in need or saying a prayer at the dinner table. Maybe it's discovered through creating something together and sharing joy in each other's passions.

> **A spiritual relationship is much, much more than just spending time together: It's about how your partnership is going to help facilitate a deeper connection to help bring out the best version of each other and to have the life the both of you want the most.**

It is the simple things that often have the most meaning, *and how the connection is made is not as important as how it makes you feel—and how that feeling spreads to those around you.* Each individual and couple has their own way to connect that will help provide a healthier and happier life, and a sense of purpose.

Chapter 17

SINGLE MOMS
Embracing the "New Normal"

While parents who are part of a couple may see their children's departure as an opportunity to rekindle the flame within their relationship (see Chapter 16), all the single moms out there may have a more difficult transition ahead (or who knows; maybe it will be even more fun).

Many single moms who play the role of both mom and dad tend to put their own social lives and goals on the back burner in order to focus on raising the children. I was a single mom for two years when my kids were young (that's not long in the "big picture," but I certainly got a taste of single life), and in those two years I can attest that every ounce of my focus (plus some!) went to the children and *their* needs. Because of the abusive relationship I endured before getting divorced, I took to heart raising (and especially protecting) my children, even when and after I remarried. For this reason, I relate somewhat to the type of relationship a single mom has with her children in comparison to the relationships that exist in two-parent families.

In single-parent families, the child and parent may rely more heavily on each other, may provide more emotional support for one another, and can be more "enmeshed" when it comes to decision-making. When I was on my own as a parent, my children and I bonded extra-close. Despite this closeness, I fully appreciated Tony's support in raising our children and providing for our family once we were married.

One mother I interviewed, Michelle, got divorced when her son Dylan and daughter Heather were in high school. She remained single and stayed strong as their lives and needs kept her extremely busy. But three years later, when Dylan went into the military and Haley went off to college, it hit Michelle especially hard. She didn't have anyone left in the house to feel strong for, and she became extremely lonely.

It's a huge life transition when the child whom a single parent has been raising for years leaves the nest.

Going from a two-person (or, three, as in Michelle's case) household to a single-person household can be a shock to the system and take some getting used to. If you are a mom who isn't a part of a couple, the empty house can seem even emptier—and lonely. As with all empty-nest moms, it's time to take care of you. This chapter of your life is a great opportunity to try new things and find out what it is *you* want!

Survival Steps

After talking with Michelle and interviewing single mothers, I found that empty-nest single moms who were happy and fulfilled did five things to help them survive the transition:

- **Make a weekly girls' night out (or in!).** Nothing feels better than to get together with good friends. It's hard to go out for a movie or a drink if you have kids in the home, but you're an empty nester now, so go out and have some fun with friends—or invite them over for a movie or dinner. Make it a weekly ritual so you can look forward to it, and to avoid the monotony of day after day, week after week, simply passing on by.

- **Clean and redecorate your space.** It's *your* home and *your* space now. Constant reminders of the past sometimes make it harder to move forward. If so, pick a room that you spend a lot of time in, and start to redecorate. You don't even have to compromise on the choices with a partner or kids—it's entirely *your* space now. So if you've always wanted to buy a purple couch, paint the walls yellow, or hang a favorite photo . . . go for it!

- **Join an online dating site.** Kids are a good excuse to hide from the dating scene, but now that you are an empty-nester, you're free to explore your options. No doubt, it will be a little scary to put yourself "out there." But it could be a lot of fun too! Michelle and her friend Jeanie had great fun at first simply browsing the online profiles of available men. They didn't accept any dates at first, but took their time and simply looked around until they were comfortable with the idea (and choices!). When they felt they were ready, they went on dates and met some really nice people.

- **Become part of a group!** Choose to reach out to others in the same situation as you. For example, Leslie gets together with fellow empty nesters for films and fun. She joined two MeetUp groups that engage in a variety of activities. Or join groups that focus on interests of yours. If you love books, research and join a book club, or if you love exercise, join a hiking, biking, or runners' club. Or become part of a community-based or neighborhood group that offers a variety of activities. If you're already engaged in some groups, use your new empty-nest status to take on a more active role in the club, such as a leadership position.

- **Start a bucket list!** Think about *before* you had kids—*what were you passionate about?* It's overwhelming to start fresh sometimes, but now you can do and see things for yourself without having to take care of anyone except you! One friend of mine went to Spain and trekked the Camino de Santiago while her daughter was away in college. This renewed her spirit, made her connect with her identity, and definitely took her mind off her single situation. Make your list and start by picking one thing . . . and then do it!

This is the time to reinvent yourself and discover untapped talents and interests. Most importantly, you can rediscover something that other single mothers (and many moms from all different living situations) often lose along the path of parenthood—your sense of self.

Conclusion

BE AUTHENTIC

The secret to a lasting and successful relationship—whether you're single or part of a couple—is *being authentic.* To be authentic simply means to be happy—*being happy with yourself.* This happiness naturally expands into other areas of your life.

A happy person is respectful, considerate, self-motivated, and goal-oriented. Egos, jealousy, control, and perfectionism do not overtake, or interfere with, a happy person and how they choose to live their life. Happy people aren't completely free of these negative emotions and tendencies, *but they don't fall victim to them.* They have an awareness that helps them rise above negative emotions and tendencies, and into a respect for self, others, and the surrounding environment.

If we lose the ability to communicate with and trust our inner selves, how can we expect to have happy and fulfilling relationships with our adult children or partners?

How we take care of and value ourselves directly influences our quality of life and any relationship with another person.

Be authentic.

Besides, it's best to be yourself because everyone else is already taken.

ABOUT THE AUTHOR

Lila Reyna is the creator of Action Awareness Training, a personal self-defense and empowerment program, and the author of several books, one of which, *Street Sense: Smart Self-Defense for Children,* landed on the USA Best Books list and won a 2016 Parent's Choice Award from *Parents' Resource Guide.*

Lila first started training in the martial art of Kuk Sool Won™ over 20 years ago, and today holds the rank of 4th Degree Black Belt. She is currently in the testing process for her Master's degree. Lila is also a practitioner of Frequency Energy Medicine™, a unique healing technique that uses specialized skills of intuition and empathy and is comprised of three major aspects: the mind, the body, and the spirit.

Based on the foundational wisdoms and practices of both traditions, Lila created Action Awareness Training to help others enhance their quality of life, personal safety and greater selves. Action Awareness Training workshops and seminars help develop powerful life skills, like the ability to confront limiting habits of behavior and thought in order to attain greater awareness.

As an abuse survivor, Lila originally entered the martial arts and healing world with a determination to reclaim her power and learn the skills to protect herself and her children. Lila learned to turn abuse from defining her to driving her to make a difference in the lives of women around the globe.

In letting her children go and be grown, she is thrilled to focus her passion on teaching awareness. Action Awareness speaking engagements, online classes, and onsite workshops are available. To sign up for her free newsletter or to bring Lila to your area, contact her at www.lilareyna.com.

Lila lives in Northern California with her husband, Tony, and their dog Hana. She converses with Hana way too much since the kids moved out.

Embrace your new life, join the journey and connect with Lila on:
Facebook: @LilaReyna
Instagram: @lila.reyna

10 things I'm Good at

1. puzzles
2. Cooking + baking
3. my job
4. Being a mom
5. Fashion
6. Being kind to others
7. Handling a crisis
8. Driving
9. Exercise
10. Recognizing good music

Weaknesses

1. Worry too much | Compassionate
2. Put others's needs in front of my own. | Selfless
3. avoid taking risks at work. | Consistent
4. Don't always say how I feel. | Empathetic
5. Put too much pressure on myself. | Perfectionist

Made in United States
North Haven, CT
05 September 2022

23699343R00129